GUIDE FOR
Parents
WITH
Careers

Sound, "parent-tested" advice and practical worksheets
to work out your concerns about:

Child Care Alternatives

How to find, select, evaluate, and monitor your child's care.

Improving Home and Time Management

So you have more time for fun and relaxation with your family.

Dual Career Couples and Single Parents

*Recognizing and controlling guilt and stress, part-time vs. full-time
work, making better decisions about stages and phases of careers.*

Other Parenting Issues

*When to go back to work, breastfeeding and working, having a
second child, and much, much more.*

GUIDE FOR
Parents
WITH
Careers

Ideas on How to Cope

Rebecca Sager Ashery, DSW, and Michele Margolin Basen, MPA

ACROPOLIS BOOKS LTD.
WASHINGTON, D.C.

Dedication

To the Basens—Barry, Ryan, Michael and Tyler
&
To the Asherys—Avy, Elie and Barak

ACROPOLIS BOOKS, LTD.
Colortone Building, 2400 17th St., N.W.
Washington, D.C. 20009

Printed in the United States of America by
COLORTONE PRESS
Creative Graphics, Inc.
Washington, D.C. 20009

Attention: Schools and Corporations
ACROPOLIS books are available at quantity discounts with bulk purchase for educational, business, or sales promotional use. For information, please write to: SPECIAL SALES DEPARTMENT, ACROPOLIS BOOKS LTD., 2400 17th ST., N.W., WASHINGTON, D.C. 20009.

Library of Congress Cataloging in Publication Data

Ashery, Rebecca Sager, 1945-
Guide for Parents with Careers
Includes index.
   1. Parenting. 2. Parents—Employment—Social aspects. 3. Day care centers—Evaluation. 4. Home economics. 5. Child rearing. I. Basen, Michele Margolin, 1949- . II. Title.
HQ755.8.A74 1986 649'.1 83-7110
ISBN 0-87491-803-0 (pbk)

The authors participated equally in the writing of this book.

Contents

time, what effort for what return?
• Putting management in your
home, types of home management,
the household manager, exclusive
domain, modified exclusive domain,
role sharing • Change charts for
food chores, home maintenance,
clothes chores, family management,
money and paper management, car
maintenance • The "like" scales
• convenience notebooks for home
management and personal and
financial matters • Home management tips, suggested files.

Career in a holding pattern • Child
versus children—having more than
one • Competition for time
• Couple communications
• Decisions—how to make them
• Does money equal tired? • Family
management and communication tips
• Getting along with mothers who
work at home • Guilt and stress
• Help—when to see an expert
• Long-distance commuting
• Marriage contracts • Nursing
and working • Parents—to be or
not to be • Part-time versus full-time
work • Pediatricians—how to
choose • Quitting a job or not
quitting • Returning to work
• Returning to work after a baby—
when is best? • Saturday night out
• Single parents • Travel on the job
• Why not fun?

Charts

Preface

We first developed Parents With Careers to provide workshops, seminars, consultation and counseling on issues related to combining work and parenting. We had both stumbled through periods of "trial and error" wondering "How do I do it?"; How can I find quality child care?"; "How do I keep from feeling guilty?" We researched the literature for answers and found it deplorable! We hate the books and magazine articles that tell you how Mary Jane returned to work and became president of the bank; or how Mary Ann, with five kids, was divorced and is now a leading fashion designer. They are exceptions. The reality is that it is tough to divide yourself between work and family. It is tough to juggle, and there are plenty who drop out for a while.

Because we found nothing to meet our needs or the needs of others, we organized the Parents With Careers workshops. We developed these workshops based on extensive research, our own personal experiences, and the experiences of friends and workshop participants. This book is based on our Parents With Careers Workshops which we provide for corporations and community groups.

The aim of the workshops and the book is to give specific information to participants which would be of immediate use to them in successfully combining working and parenting. This book is meant to be used. It contains dozens of tear-out charts to aid parents in assessing their choices. It provides formulas to help readers put the charts in perspective and evaluate their findings about issues like child care.

We feel we have succeeded in our goal of dealing in a rational manner with the mind boggling problems associated with working and maintaining a family. We've had positive feedback on the usefulness of our worksheets, checklists, and practical suggestions from the hundreds of participants who have taken our workshops. We hope we can help even more individuals who read our book.

We want you to keep in mind as you use this book that it is difficult to pioneer new territory and develop new roles and lifestyles, particularly when "the territory" (your children, your job, yourself) keeps changing. But it can be done, with cooperation and perseverance. You may not become the bank president or a leading fashion designer. But you can have a job you like, a lifestyle you enjoy, and a satisfying relationship with your children and your family.

We would like to hear feedback from you regarding our book and practical suggestions which have worked for you.

Introduction

You don't have time for extracurricular reading, so don't read this book—use it! Detach the relevant charts. They will help you to:

- Understand the advantages and disadvantages of various types of child care
- Personalize your child-care decisions
- More intelligently select child care
- Monitor your child care—and make changes when necessary
- Prevent problems inherent to child care
- Develop household notebooks and have important information at your fingertips
- Decide which home management responsibilities are most and least important; when they should be done and how often they should be done
- Decide who should take responsibility for particular household chores
- Organize your home management responsibilities using a household chart
- Take advantage of tips that have been tested by other working parents
- Handle problems related to parents with careers, such as scheduling, communication, and role conflict
- Diminish feelings of stress and guilt
- Make decisions about career mobility that are in concert with your family's needs, your goals, and the ages and development of your children
- Consider the advantages and disadvantages of part-time versus full-time work
- Increase your chances of successfully working and nursing
- And more!

The charts, worksheets, tips, and hints are especially designed for busy parents who may have liked some of the practical suggestions they have heard about before but never had time to implement them. Now, they are all laid out for you. Just fill in the blanks.

ASHERY

Child Care

- The books said your newborn would sleep 18 hours a day, but it's just the opposite. You're exhausted. Your boss wants to know when you'll be back to work.
- Your three-year-old is bored staying at home with the wonderful housekeeper it took you so long to find.
- Your caretaker just announced that she's moving overseas.
- Your new job is in the opposite direction of the day-care center.

Child care is usually the issue of immediate concern to working parents. You have probably already observed and talked with friends and co-workers whose situations are similar to yours. But each family situation is unique. You must ultimately make a decision regarding child care based on the special needs of your child (for example, age, adaptability, sleep patterns, health records) and family needs (such as financial limitations, working hours, flexibility, marital status, available resources).

And, as soon as you think you have worked it all out, something will change! Remember, children, sitters, and jobs or careers grow and change. The child care arrangements you have for your infant most likely will not meet the needs of a toddler. Your suburban office may move downtown. And your reliable sitter may decide she wants a higher-paying job. Don't panic. The name of the game is *change* and *flexibility*. We should keep this in mind as we examine child care alternatives.

Child-Care Alternatives

There are essentially five major types of child care. Please remember that regulations involving family day care, day-care centers, and nursery schools are different in various jurisdictions. Usually the county and state departments of social service, health and education are involved in their regulation. Check with these departments by calling county and state information numbers in your areas.

Remember, too, when you hire a caregiver, you become an employer subject to federal and state laws relating to compensation and benefits. See IRS Form #940 (Employers Annual Federal Unemployment Tax Returns) and IRS Publication #503 (Children and Disabled Dependent Care).

Family Day Care. Laws regulating family day care vary in different areas. Essentially, family day care is provided for a fee in someone's home. The day-care mother often cares for more than one child in her home—and may have her own children also. Many areas regulate the number of children, require licensing and inspections, and provide workshops on day care. Family day care is the most common form of child care and is usually the least costly. Some areas provide subsidies to help offset costs to parents.

Day woman to your home means someone comes to your home on a regular basis to care for your children. *Live-in help* lives in your home full- or part-time with set hours available to you for child care. In both cases their responsibilities may or may not include housekeeping. The full responsibility for screening and monitoring this type of care lies with you.

Day care centers provide care on a regular basis for a larger number of children (often, ten or more) than a family day-care home. In many areas a child must be two years old before attending a center, but some areas have day-care centers for infants. Such infant centers (newborn to 24 months) stipulate a strict ratio of staff to children (often 1:4 or 1:3 for less than 12 months), stricter safety precautions, specified age-appropriate activities, a separate room for the day care, and where possible, consistent assignment of the same staff to each group of four children. As you would expect, costs are higher. Care for children is usually provided by well-trained staff with designated qualifications. For all centers, staff-child ratios, types of equipment, and environment are variables which are controlled by regulation.

Pre-school nursery program with extended day components (morning and afternoon) are similar to day-care centers, in terms of activities and scheduling. They may also be subject to licensing by the board of education.

Boards of education frequently specify more stringent administrative and faculty qualifications, activities, and student-teacher ratios than day-care centers. They also require written policies. A day-care center and a nursery school with an extended-day component may be very similar, or they may be very different—depending on local regulations.

Chart 1 on page 5 shows the pros and cons of each child care alternative discussed above.

Family day care is the most prevalent and least expensive kind of child care. If a day-care mother is licensed, you have the assurance that someone else has done some screening, but don't rely on this entirely. Most agencies are overburdened and the licensing requirements are minimal. Your child gets the advantage of personalized attention and also the stimulation of having other children around. S/he is part of a small social group (usually anywhere from one to six children, perhaps varying in age). The background and experience of family day care mothers vary, and the kinds of equipment, stimulation and affection provided vary with the person involved. Many, however, consider themselves to be dedicated professionals and are usually experienced raising their own children. The relationship between parent and day care mother is one of mutual cooperation.

However, you must remember that since the day care is conducted in the day care mother's home, she may or may not be willing to honor all of your suggestions. She is hiring you as much as you are hiring her since she wants a mother that she is compatible with and wants a child that will fit into her current group of children. She sets the rates, the kind of schedule that is convenient for her, and the activities that she does with the children. She will have her own way of disciplining children in her home. She may allow the children to do things that you would not allow in your home, or vice versa.

With live-ins and day women you have the advantage of in-home care. You don't have to take a young child out on a snowy morning; you often have the added benefit of someone doing housework and being in the home for other household matters, such as visits from the plumber. You can't take an ill child to family day care and expose other children, but you can keep the child home with a day woman or live-in. Also, many day women must depend on public transportation. A late arrival could affect your work schedule. And, while live-ins and day women are generally more convenient they are also more costly in salary and hidden expenses like utilities and food. And it is more difficult to find good help. There appears to be higher turnover among live-ins and day women than among family day-care mothers who may have a professional commitment to the job.

The Preschooler

When looking at schools and day-care centers, you are usually considering a stimulating environment for a two- to four-year-old child. Unlike nursery schools, which frequently follow public-school schedules, day-care centers are usually open longer hours and have provisions for summer programs and vacation days. Many day-care centers provide a "nursery school curriculum" during the course of the day. Ratios, teachers, programs, and environment must be checked carefully. (See the section on evaluating schools and centers.)

The Infant

Many parents who return to work when their children are very young, find it most difficult to find quality in-home care. As mentioned above, some jurisdictions have now modified their laws to allow for strictly regulated infant care within day-care centers. While there are many advantages to keeping your infant at home, the following are the advantages to an infant day-care center:

- Parent has access to, and support of other parents and professionals
- Standards for centers are high and requirements encourage hiring of good, experienced staff (qualities looked for include warmth, patience, energy, good health).
- It has been found that infants and toddlers *do* respond positively to other children under controlled circumstances
- Infants and toddlers are exposed to several, but consistent role models
- Infants and toddlers are exposed early to cultural differences

Other options. A less prevalent form of child care is "group care." It can best be understood as a step between family day care and a day-care center.

(continued on page 7)

CHART 1: Child-Care Alternatives: Pros and Cons

Type of Care	I. Family Day Care	II. Live-In Help	III. Babysitter Coming
Advantages	Some licensed Most have children of their own One caring adult Least costly; sliding scale Stimulation of other children Extended family Some have flexible hours	No early morning hassle Child's illness—less problem Often does house-keeping, too More flexible hours Good for more than one child More control as employer	Often does house-keeping, too Child's illness—less problem Good for more than one child More control as employer
Disadvantages	Licensing focuses chiefly on environment, not social, psychological considerations Taking child out in bad weather Illness (on both sides) Less convenient when you have more than one child Relationship between parent and caregiver one of mutual cooperation —some loss of control as an employer	Costly Family gives up some privacy May be "undocumented worker"—some legal issues Hidden expenses (utilities, food) Often must deal with personal problems of employee Possible language limitations Difficult to find good help Turnover Fewer children for stimulation and company	Transportation diffi-culties (if bus is late bringing your sitter, then you will be late, too) Difficult to find good help Hidden expenses (utilities, food) Turnover Fewer children for stimulation and company

CHART 1: Child-Care Alternatives: Pros and Cons (continued)

Type of Care	IV. Day-Care Center	V. Nursery School Programs
Advantages	Child has experience with other children; socialization	Geared toward cognitive development—within 2-3 hour period
	Planned activities (some cognitive) spread through whole day	Child has experience with other children
	Long hours, seldom closed	Sometimes offer special services
	Continuity of program	
	Sometimes offer special services	
Disadvantages	No provision for illness	No provision for illness
	Taking young child out of home in bad weather	More costly than day care
	Long day in non-home environment	Taking young child out of home in bad weather
		May not have summer arrangements or vacation day arrangements

In group care there are usually more than six children, with an additional day-care mother or aide, but they remain in a home environment. Sometimes these arrangements are informal—an agreement between day-care mothers and parents—and sometimes these arrangements are formalized through a licensing procedure. A few states do license "group care." The advantages of this type of child care are similar to those for family day care: a home environment, the parent has more control over the situation, and more flexible hours. Also, children of differing ages are accepted, it's generally more economical, the children benefit from the stimulation of other children, and have the continuity of a regular care-giver (a mother). Of course the disadvantages of family day care also apply: if unlicensed, these homes are subject to no screening. All the selecting and monitoring must be the responsibility of the parent. And many of these group day-care mothers are untrained. You must question carefully their qualifications and schedule of activities. You must inspect the house and surrounding environment very carefully.

A relatively rare but growing form of child care is employer-sponsored child care. Both employers and labor unions can support child care through varied means, including:

- Providing information, through workshops and seminars
- Providing financial assistance to parents or to existing programs in the form of vouchers for care or the purchase of slots in a center
- Developing programs for on-site or off-site care

Many employers make information available about child-care services, either directly through their own workshops and seminars or indirectly, by agreement with an outside agency. This is probably the most common form of child-care involvement by an employer; it takes the fewest resources on the part of the employer. Yet it can be most advantageous, particularly to a family that has recently relocated and needs to make child-care decisions rapidly.

A few companies have donated money or other resources to existing child-care centers or family day-care centers to allow for extension of services to their employees. A company can also reach an agreement with a center to purchase a certain number of slots for their employees, or to subsidize the employee's cost by paying for part of a slot at a designated site.

Or, an employer can supply vouchers to an employee for a specific amount of child care at no designated site.

A few employers have become involved in child care to a greater extent by actually developing new child-care programs. Several large firms have developed on-site or off-site centers, and assumed all of the responsibilities for administration, hiring, licensing, and costs. A related commitment is that of a consortium child-care center, where a number of employers agree to share resources, liability, and costs for an off-site, mutually convenient child-care center.

As you would expect, there are a number of variations on these major types, and a number of advantages and disadvantages to each. It is generally agreed, though, that these innovations are on the increase. If you'd like further information on the subject of employer-supported child care, we suggest: "Employers and Child Care: Establishing Services Through the Workplace," published by the U.S. Department of Labor (Office of the Secretary, Women's Bureau. Revised August 1982. Pamphlet #23).*

Combination of care. You may consider a combination of alternatives. For example, you may send your child to half-day nursery school and have a day-care mother, live-in help, or a day woman for the afternoon hours (if you can arrange car pools).

Choosing the type of child care is your first hurdle. Chart 1 will help you decide among the five prevalent types of child care.

HINT: Don't forget, when you pay for care for a child while you are working or looking for work, you can get a tax credit. See IRS Form 2441 (Credit for Child and Dependent Care Expenses).

Latch-Key Children

At what age can children be trusted to stay at home alone after school?

The maturity of your child is more important than the chronological age. You must make a judgment about maturity. If the school or recreation center in your neighborhood offers an after-school program, we strongly

*Send a self-addressed mailing label to the Women's Bureau, Room S3005, U.S. Department of Labor, Washington, D.C. 20210 (for single copies only).

suggest that your child attend. Your peace of mind is important. If there is no such program, look for teenagers or day-care mothers who are walking distance from home or school. If none of these options are available, and your child must be at home alone, we feel that age ten is an appropriate age for a child to stay home alone. But rules must be set up and obeyed:

- May your child go out and play? Where? For how long?
- May your child have friends over?
- May she or he turn on the oven? Use other appliances?
- May your child watch television? What programs?
- Is he or she expected to do homework?
- Does your child have your phone number? Have the child call you at a set time each day.
- Does your child know how to call an emergency number?
- Is there a neighbor who can check in sometimes?
- Is your neighborhood relatively safe?
- Will your child be responsible for younger siblings? How young? Do they generally get along well together? Does the younger sibling understand the rules and that the older one is in charge?

Suggestion: If you are worried about your child's walk home either from school or the bus stop, consider hiring an older child to walk your child home.

Now that you have examined the pros and cons chart, examine your child's and family's needs on the Guide on page 10.

Locating Child Care

Once you have decided on the type of care, measures must be taken to locate it. There are numerous resources for this, depending upon your locale. Some counties and cities have special booklets prepared by an office for child care (or comparable department). Try your library for these booklets. Often you will be provided with lists of caretakers by geographic location and other variables, such as the ages of children accepted. Thankfully, some counties have purchased computers, and a great deal of information can be obtained through one telephone call.

Guide: Picture Yourself and Your Family and Consider: What Are Your Family's Needs, Interests, Limitations?

Ages of children?

- How much socialization do you desire at each age?
- How mobile are your children at each age?

Your child's experiences?

- How much contact with other children?
- How much discipline and permissiveness is the child accustomed to and what is the child's behavior?
- Much illness?
- How adaptable is the child?

How flexible are you?

- Your work hours?
- Can you participate in child care?
- Location of your job, child care, your home?

What can you afford?

What is available in your area?

Your philosophy of early childhood—what kinds of experiences and atmosphere do you want?

Remember: Change is inevitable!

Do not rely solely on such a service. If registration is voluntary in your jurisdiction, there may be many fine caretakers who are not registered. Use a broad survey method, and begin making inquiries yourself. First, use your personal network: ask relatives, friends, co-workers, neighbors. Call the local nursery schools, hospitals, and day-care centers to inquire if they know of caretakers. Post ads on community bulletin boards, at doctors' offices, health clinics, churches, and synagogues, and in newsletters for local children's, women's, and elderly groups. A newspaper ad is most helpful, and not too costly, if you are specific. Include:

- Number and ages of children
- Hours and days required
- Area you live in
- Type of care desired (housework and babysitting)
- Other special requirements (for example, car necessary, nonsmoker)
- Phone number

Don't waste your money and time with: "Wanted: mature, loving, responsible adult . . . . " Every caretaker feels she is mature, responsible and loving. You must screen for these qualities yourself.

Before we discuss *how* to screen efficiently, another hint: *Don't plan too far in advance.* People who answer these ads usually are looking for an immediate job. You cannot agree to hire someone and then keep the person on hold until your child is three months old or your maternity leave is over. A good rule of thumb: allow about two months for finding child care.

Screening

Once you have advertised, you will want to screen your telephone responses and their references. Hang Charts 2, 3 and 4 (page 13) (with extra copies) by your telephone. You will find them valuable.

If the respondent sounds good during your telephone screening conversation, obtain references with phone numbers. To save time and energy, contact the references prior to making an appointment for an in-person interview with the prospective employee. Often someone may sound fine over the telephone, but previous employers give a different picture.

Tell the prospective employee, "You sound like a good candidate for the job. I am checking references before conducting interviews. May I have the names and telephone number of people you have worked for?" Then explain you are doing telephone screening. "Depending on the number of applicants and their qualifications, I may or may not be contacting your references. I will call you within a week should I decide an interview would be appropriate." This gives you control of the conversation and lets the caller know what to expect.

It is particularly important to record your impressions as soon as you hang up. You may find yourself besieged with phone calls and unable to recall your impressions at the time of an in-person interview. Try to listen for *the callers' responses.* Give *them* an opportunity for questions. This will give you a good idea of their initiative and interest. You might also find it useful to keep a set of index cards and a calendar by the telephone.

More on References

Try to call references as soon as possible if you think you have a good job candidate.

You may ask yourself how to respond to a mediocre reference. Listen carefully and try to probe. The applicant may have had difficulty controlling the reference's six-year-old boy, but how would she do with your infant? Ask the reference's opinion. Maybe the applicant was terrible at doing laundry; however, laundry is not one of your household requirements. If the reference rates the applicant's housecleaning as "average," what does average mean?

Never reveal to an applicant what a reference has told you. If an applicant asks if you have checked her references, do not lie. You may say "Yes, but we have decided to hire someone with more experience; or someone who lives closer by."

Reference Letters

Another cross-check on an individual is a reference letter. An applicant may bring such a letter to the interview. Learn to read between the lines.

Here is an example of a reference letter that appears good on the

(continued on page 21)

CHART 2: How to Conduct a Telephone Screening Interview for a Child-Care Applicant (Day Woman or Live-In)

Date of Telephone call _____

Name of applicant _____

Address of applicant _____ Phone _____

1. Introduce yourself
2. Confirm purpose of call ("Are you answering my ad in the *Washington Post*/on the bulletin board in the clinic?")
3. Ask the following questions:
   - Are you working now?

   - What type of work?

   - Where was your last job? What was the name, phone number, and address of current and most recent employer?

   - How long were you at current or most recent job?

   - What was reason for leaving?

   - What previous jobs have you had? How long have you stayed with them? For jobs related to child care, what was the reason for leaving?

CHART 2: How to Conduct a Telephone Screening Interview for a Child-Care Applicant (Day Woman or Live-in) (continued)

- What kinds of things do you like to do with children?

- What sort of activities would a child (of age ____) like to take part in?

- Do you have children? What are their ages? What arrangements for child care do you have?

- How old are you?

- What would be your transportation?

- Ask for references, including name, address, and phone of previous employers and others.

4. Impressions: Listen to questions *they* ask you. Did they hesitate? Were they prepared to answer your questions regarding what kinds of things they like to do with children?

Hint: Hang photo copies of this list by your telephone.

CHART 3: How to Conduct A Telephone Screening Interview For A Child Care Applicant (Family Day Care)

Date of Telephone call _____

Name of applicant _____

Address of applicant _____ Phone _____

1. Introduce yourself

2. Confirm purpose of call (The county licensing office gave me your name; I saw your name on the church bulletin board)

3. Ask the following questions:
   - How long have you been doing day care in your home?

   - Have you had jobs outside the home which involved care of children? Type of work? When? How many years worked?

   - Any jobs outside the home not involving children? Type of work? When? How many years worked?

   - Do you have children of your own? How old are they?

CHART 3: **How to Conduct a Telephone Screening Interview for a Child Care Applicant (Family Day Care) (continued)**

- How many children are you caring for now? (excluding your own) What are their ages?

- Do you care for them full time/part time?

- Do you care for children all year around? How long do you ususally take off for summer vacation?

- What is the layout of your house? Do you have a special playroom for the children? Where do they sleep?

- Describe briefly a typical day with the children in your care.

- What kinds of activities do you do with the children in your care?

- What happens if you are sick? Do you have back up help?

- Do you have any special stipulations in running your family day care home or in taking care of children such as required naps, T.V. watching?

- Are you willing to cooperate regarding the special needs of my child such as diet, medication?

- What are your fees?

- What are your hours?

- How old are you?

- References—name, address, and phone number of parents whose children are currently or have been previously in your care.

4. Impression: Listen to questions *they* ask you. Did they hesitate? Were they prepared to answer your questions regarding what kinds of things they like to do with children?

Hint: Hang photo copies of this list by your telephone.

CHART 4: How to Conduct a Telephone Interview with a Reference

Date of Telephone call _____

Name of applicant _____

Address of applicant _____ Phone _____

1. Introduce yourself

2. Confirm identity of the reference ("Is this so and so?")

3. Ask the following questions:

   • How long did applicant work for you? Dates of employment.

   • If in capacity of child care, what ages were your children during that period?

   • What were reasons for termination?

   • What type of work was required (housework, child care, work hours, specific responsibilities, other responsibilities?)

   • How much did you pay?

   • What were the applicant's previous jobs?

- Did you check for references?

- What were the applicants' strong points?

- Weak points?

- Would you choose this person again?

- What did you like most or least about this person?

4. Impressions: Did reference hesitate, sound at all cautious?

(continued from page 12)

surface, but reflects hesitation on the part of the former employer. You should talk personally with the employer as there may be things she does not want to put in writing.

To Whom It May Concern:

Jane Doe has worked for us for the past year. During that time her responsibilities included housekeeping and child care for my three-year-old son. She is very dependable—always arriving on time even in the most treacherous weather and only missed three days of work because of illness during the entire year. My son is fond of her.

Sincerely,
Mary Smith

What do you think of this letter? What does/doesn't this letter tell you about Jane Doe? You need to know:

- More about her responsibilities
- Personality—is she pleasant, moody?
- How did the child respond to her?
- Evaluation of her work
- Why is she no longer working there?
- Would reference hire her again?
- Does reference recommend her to others?

Here is another reference letter giving more details about Jane Doe's employment:

To Whom It May Concern:

Jane Doe has worked for me for the past year. During that time her responsibilities included housekeeping and child care for my three-year-old son. This included typical household chores such as vacuuming, laundry, dusting, dishes, etc. She was responsible for bathing, feeding, playing stimulating games with my three-year-old, and taking him outdoors in good weather. She is very dependable, always arriving on time even in the most treacherous weather and only missed three days of work because of illness during the entire year. She is a very pleasant person to have in the house and she did an excellent job. My son is very fond of her. My son is now entering a full-day nursery school, and I will no longer need Ms. Doe's services. Should the occasion arise I would not hesitate to hire Ms. Doe again. I would highly recommend her for employment. If you have any questions you can call me at 882-3704.

Sincerely,
Mary Smith

In-Person Interview for Day-Care Mother, Live-in or Day Woman

Probably the most difficult part of finding child care is the actual interview. Not many of us have had direct experience with interviewing applicants for a job. When the job is taking care of your young child, the task can seem formidable.

A few pointers. First, expect that a good percent of your scheduled interviewees won't show up for the appointment. Consider it a good screening technique. Once you do settle down for your interviews, take control. Many experienced caretakers recognize a young, anxious parent and tend to dictate their requirements. It is always helpful to have another point of view on childrearing, and to recognize any of the candidate's limitations before hiring. However, it is *your* child. You must be clear about your requirements.

Use the following checklist (Chart 5, page 23) during the interview.

HINTS:

- Have at least two interviews prior to hiring any applicant.

- For day-care mothers: Interview her by yourself the first time. You can observe how she deals with the children in her care. If satisfied, bring your child on a second visit and observe for an hour or so.

- For live-in or day woman: Even though it may add some confusion, try to have your children around for the initial interview. Observe how the applicant relates to them. If you are satisfied, have her come for a second interview. Have her stay for a few hours (you should pay her for her time) and observe her care of your child and handling of household situations. You may even leave for a short time.

- Overlap with caretaker. If at all possible there should be a two-week overlap between the time your caretaker's responsibility begins and the time you go back to work. This is a good "settling in" time to handle any problems which may arise. It can also be a training period for the

(continued on page 25)

CHART 5: How to Interview a Day-Care Mother, Live-In or Day Woman

Interview Checklist

1. Question applicant's background.
   - Previous child-care experience, e.g., number and ages of children cared for (for each job), references, dates of employment, reasons for termination
   - Other jobs, e.g., describe, length of employment, reasons for termination
   - Family and other current responsibilities
   - If day-care mother, does she appear to be organized and able to respond to the needs of several children?
   - Question current health

2. Describe specific responsibilities.
   - Hours of child care
   - Activities with child, such as bathing, taking walks, feeding lunch
   - Housekeeping: laundry, cooking, light or heavy cleaning, etc.
   - For day-care mother, care of your child in relation to other children; how many day care children are present each day, morning and afternoon? (This often varies and too much change can be confusing for child).
   - For day-care mother, do other children seem happy, busy?
   - For day-care mother, are ages of other children compatible with your child?

3. Review daily schedule to facilitate communications between caretaker, parents, and children.
   - Transportation
   - Time to be spent with your child, with house, with other children

4. Review special issues of childrearing.
   - Discipline techniques
   - Nutrition
   - Television watching
   - Naps

5. Discuss and negotiate pay and leave policies.
   - Salary, when paid, social security and other monetary benefits
   - Paid vacations, sick leave
   - Provision of back-up sitters (you will want to interview day care mother's backup sitter).

6. Observe home and discuss equipment needs (for day-care mother).
   - Is home neat, organized, safe?
   - Who provides baby equipment, food, diapers, toys?
   - Where will your child sleep? Is family living area separate from day-care play area?
   - Are toys and equipment appropriate to children's ages?

7. Review special instructions.
   - Medications, emergency plans, emergency phone numbers
   - Special schedules, rules of the house, e.g., if nonsmoker, family pets
   - Special nutritional, religious requirements
   - Someone to rely on for emergencies

(continued from page 22)

caretaker to learn your household while you are there, and for you to more thoroughly observe her interaction with your children.

We have heard that even after extensive interviews and reference-checking an employee hired may not show up for the job on the first day. Make sure you keep a backup list of second and third choices. The overlap period will give you time to find another caretaker.

Overall: *Trust your instincts!*

Let's say you have narrowed your list to two individuals. Take a look at both of them.

Person A

- Age 35

- Has young child in school

- Has worked for two other families in the past five years with some gaps—other employment was sales work

- Good reference from one of two families (other family moved—no reference)

- Warm, friendly toward your toddler

- Arrives late to interview (blames public transportation)

Person B

- Age 50

- Worked years ago as caretaker—recently decided to return to work

- Somewhat stiff with your toddler

- References good—but not with child-care experiences

- Arrives promptly—asks intelligent questions

Whom Do You Choose?

Examine the situation. Perhaps Person A had gaps in employment due to her own child's needs and sales work was something she could do part-time. Ask her. Perhaps she was late because the bus line had changed, or it was on a holiday schedule. (Don't roll your eyes, it happened to Michele on her first day back to work—Columbus Day—and her wonderful sitter has now been with her for two years). Ask her what kind of after-school care she has for her own child. What will she do when her child is sick? Is Person B a "youthful" age 50? Perhaps she was stiff with your toddler due to interview stress (we all know what that is). Maybe she has raised her own family. Ask her about this experience. Are some of her previous job skills transferrable to child care?

The point of this exercise? Have another interview with each. It will be well worth your time.

If you are still feeling a bit overwhelmed, try having someone sit in with you during the interview. Or try summarizing the information you have on each caretaker, with a summary sheet (Chart 6A, page 29).

Hiring

The following is an example of a written agreement, of the job responsibilities and "personnel policy" that you and your employee agree upon. Prior to hiring your employee (live-in or day woman), you should go over this agreement with her. She may ask for some modifications. If you can, without jeopardizing your needs, make those changes. One copy of this written agreement should be given to the employee, one copy you keep, and one copy is attached to the refrigerator. By having something in writing there will be no disagreements later regarding your verbal discussions.

You may note that in this section we use the term employer and employee. This is exactly what you are, an employer. Your relationship with your employee, while friendly, should also be professional. Hiring an employee for your child should be done in a professional manner just like hiring an employee at the office. Never forget this, and above all remember that your needs as an employer should be met.

Day-care mothers probably have their own "policies" regarding payment and vacation. Ask for these in writing. You may also write up an agreement with her on some of the particular points which meet your needs. As stated previously, the relationship is one of mutual cooperation rather than employer/employee.

Agreement Between Mary Brown (employer) and Jane Doe (employee)

Job Responsibilities

Care for one-year-old child
- Feed child breakfast, lunch, two snacks

- Bathe once per day
- Take for walk at least once per day
- Play games, provide stimulating environment
- Keep activities chart (see page 63)

General Housekeeping

- Vacuum upstairs and downstairs twice a week, vacuum basement once a week.
- Clean bathrooms once a week.
- Clean kitchen every day—wash kitchen floor as needed.
- Change sheets in master bedroom weekly.
- Change sheets in children's bedroom once a week or more if needed.
- Dust once a week.
- Water plants once a week.
- Clean woodwork once a week.
- Laundry once a week—iron if necessary.
- Empty garbage (kitchen every day—rest of house twice a week.)
- Other general housekeeping responsibilities as they occur.

Food Preparation

Every day prepare meals for child; set table for dinner; heat up food previously prepared by employer for dinner; make salad.

Hours of employment—8 A.M. to 4 P.M., Monday–Friday.

Salary

$5.00 an hour, $40 per day. Salary will paid on Friday afternoon of each week by check. (This is example. Rates vary widely by area. Also day care mothers usually charge less.)

Benefits

Employer's share of social security will be paid. Employee's share will be taken out of paycheck.

Sick Leave

One day a month—can be accumulated for sick leave during the year (no carryover to the next year).

Paid Vacation

- Two weeks paid vacation at the end of one year
- Two days paid vacation at Thanksgiving (Thursday and Friday)
- Three days paid vacation at Christmas (December 24, 25 and 26)
- Good Friday, paid vacation

This agreement is open for renegotiation at anytime between employee and employer.

Dismissal

The employee is subject to dismissal without advance notice.

*   *   *   *

How children of employed mothers compare to children of nonemployed mothers

The most common source of guilt for working parents is the feeling that they are somehow harming their children by placing them in day care. These feelings were supported by the pronouncements of many psychologists and psychiatrists that young children would suffer without their mothers' constant attention. With the recent increase in numbers of women returning to work and leaving their children in the care of others, these specialists have gone back to the drawing board. They have begun to document the longer-term effects of child care on children. Results of these recent studies disprove the earlier findings. To the question, "Is it essential for one parent to remain home during a child's early years?", the answer according to most experts is now "no."* In brief, there is little evidence that the social-emotional or intellectual well-being of children is threatened by day care. There are almost no constant differences found between children of employed and unemployed mothers.** Also, children are found to continue to prefer their parents over their caretakers, even where strong

*Edward F. Zigler and Edmund W. Gordon, eds., *Day Care: Scientific and Social Policy Issues* (Auburn House, 1982).

** Dr. Mary C. Howell, Professor of Pediatrics and Associate Dean, Harvard Medical School.

(continued on page 31)

CHART 6A: Summary Sheet—Child-Care Applicants

Name of Applicant	Transpor-tation	References	Child-Care Experience	Language	Rigid/At Ease	Salary requested	Interview impression
1	Own car	OK reference, not child care	Has 2 grown children no child-care job	articulate	at ease, warm, and friendly	average	good
2	Bus—one line, reliable	Good child care reference	1 job 2 years ago, current job unrelated	articulate	stiff, reserved	average	OK
3	2 buses	Excellent child-care reference	2 child care jobs both long-term	articulate	at ease, but cool	barely affordable	good

CHART 6B: Summary Sheet—Child-Care Applicants

Name of applicant	Transpor-tation	References	Child-care experience	Language	Rigid/At Ease	Salary requested	Interview impression
1							
2							
3							

(continued from page 28)

emotional bonds are formed with the caretaker. Moreover, there is no compelling evidence that the working mother spends less time in direct interaction with the child than does the nonworking mother.

You must realize, however, that this does not mean day care makes no difference. Children experiencing day care (here meaning care outside of the home) were found to be less cooperative with adults, more physically active, and more aggressive than at-home children. They were judged to be more active and out-going toward children their own age. These findings are not necessarily positive or negative. And of course, these findings are tempered by the kind and quality of day care experienced. Feel comfortable, though, that child development experts agree: there is no overall negative impact on a child in a good day-care situation.

Questions and Answers on Caretakers

The following are typical questions you may have about child-care providers. Our answers are based on personal experiences and those of workshop participants.

Q. *Should I contact an employment agency to obtain a day woman or live-in help?*

A. We have mixed feelings about this. Check with your friends to see what their experiences have been with local agencies. Also, check with the local better-business bureau. Some agencies are middlemen to get you and the employee together, but do no employee screening. Others screen potential employees. Even if they do, it is imperative that you also check references. Before obtaining the services of an employment agency ask them these questions:

1. Have they interviewed the applicant in person?

2. Have they interviewed the applicant's references by phone or in person—and how many were interviewed?

3. Can they give you the applicant's references?

4. Can they give you references of other people who have used the agency's services? What is the agency fee? If a fee is required, can they guarantee that the employee will stay at least 90 days?

Q. *Can I ask for a year's commitment from my child-care provider?*

A. You may ask and you may get it, but whether the arrangement will work is another story. You may ask what her future plans are, for example, whether she plans to go back to school or how long she plans to stay in this country. This will give you an idea about the future, but extracting promises is useless. After all, you don't know where you'll be in a year either!

Q. *Should I hire a non-English-speaking caretaker for my child?*

A. Many parents are concerned that their child will become confused by hearing two languages. Most likely they will not. Many children in Europe and other countries around the world grow up with two or three languages. Children have an ear for language and usually pick up a language faster than an adult. You should, however, make sure that your caretaker can handle emergencies. Can she call for an ambulance and make herself understood? Some communities have a foreign-language speaker available at the emergency number. Check in your community. Can she call you at the office and explain briefly a problem such as your child is ill. (You might also clue in your office that if someone calls with a foreign accent and mispronounces your name, it is your caretaker and not the wrong number.) We also suggest that you determine her motivation to learn the English language.

Q. *Should I hire an undocumented worker as a day woman or live-in?**

A. There are many undocumented workers (often referred to as "illegal aliens") in this country without the proper visa or "work papers." There is a procedure set up by the U.S. Department of Labor through which they can become "lawful permanent residents" (with a "green card"). This procedure usually takes a year or two. It is called an Application for Alien Employment Certification or "labor certification." It is suggested that you at least consult with an immigration attorney if you plan to hire or consider "sponsoring" an undocumented worker since these matters can be complex. For example, if the "labor certification" is approved and an I-140 Petition (Petition to Classify Preference Status of Alien on Basis of Profession or Occupation) is filed at the Immigration and Naturalization Service without waiting for the visa number or "quota," INS will probably start a deportation proceeding.

In some states it is against the law to hire a person who does not have specific "employment authorization" from the U.S. Immigration

*Special thanks to Laurence F. Johnson attorney-at-law, for his advice on this section.

and Naturalization Service. It is unknown whether, or to what extent, these state laws have been enforced against employers hiring household help. We suggest that you check with a local immigration attorney regarding the law and practices in your state. There is no national law prohibiting employers from hiring undocumented workers, although major revisions are currently proposed. U.S. law does require that employers withhold and pay social security (FICA) and pay the minimum wage (now $3.35 an hour). Contact your local IRS office for Publication 13 and Form 942. If the employee has no social security number, pay anyway putting the word "none" where the number is requested. These are filed alphabetically.

Undocumented workers have come here to make a better life for themselves, and some are fleeing persecution. Many are sending money home to support loved ones. (It should be noted that they are usually not taking jobs away from an American, because Americans are accepting other kinds of work as they move up the economic ladder.) They often come from large families and can usually take excellent care of infants and toddlers. Several words of caution, however:

References. Many of these workers have just entered the country and will not have references. They may contact a nonprofit agency (usually under church auspices) in your area to help them locate a job; or they may respond to your newspaper ad; or they may be the cousin of your friend's housekeeper. We've known people who have hired workers with no references. Some have been successful, others have not. It's luck. All the more reason to have a time when both you and your caretaker are at your home before you return to work.

Use of household appliances. Many of these workers have not had experience working in an American house. They need to be trained to operate the machinery that we take for granted: washing machines, dryers, stoves, blenders, toasters. They also need to be trained in the use of household products. If you hire an unseasoned housekeeper, you could have a trial period of two months during which her salary could initially be lower. After this probationary period, her pay should be raised for satisfactory work.

Q. *I would like to have a live-in housekeeper, but I am concerned about a loss of privacy. Is this a problem?*

A. It is true that you will lose privacy; however, it can be kept to a minimum if you follow these suggestions.

What is the layout of your house? Is it conducive to privacy for both your housekeeper and yourself? A nice furnished room in the basement with a private bathroom is ideal. Privacy can be more complicated if all of the bedrooms are on the same floor, but don't let that deter you. If you have only one bathroom, this can become uncomfortable for all involved.

Your housekeeper should help serve dinner, but she should not eat at the table with you. Dinner is private family conversation time. However, she should be available if you need her to help with the children during the dinner hour.

When she has completed her work (kitchen cleanup after dinner), she should go to her room. She should not be sitting in your family room watching television with you. Most employers provide an extra television for the housekeeper's room. (This is not a gift to her, it belongs to you for her use.) Most housekeepers usually understand these unwritten, unspoken rules, although you may have to discuss them with her. You may, however, wish to include her in some family activities such as an outing to the ice cream parlor, or McDonald's. If the above conditions are met, do not let the privacy issue be a deterrent to hiring a live-in.

Q. *I have interviewed several caretakers, who all seemed very good. I have made my selection. How do I tell the others that they did not get the job?*

A. During interviews you should let the applicants know approximately when you will be making a decision. Then all of the applicants interviewed should be called regarding your decision, since they deserve to know where they stand. Telling someone that she didn't get a job is difficult. Try to keep things upbeat and positive:

"Hello, Mrs. Cooper, this is Mrs. Green. You came to my house to interview for the child-care job last week. I was very impressed with your credentials, but I have decided to select someone else." (You don't have to go into the reasons.) "I would like to keep your name in my file for future reference." (In case something does not work out with your selection.) "If any of my friends are seeking child-care help, I will be happy to recommend that they interview you."

Q. *I have interviewed a number of caretakers, and no one has pleased me. Any suggestions?*

A. Keep looking! Keep advertising. Someone will come along. We know people who had several caretakers before they found someone they liked. Try to avoid this situation. You don't want too much change for your child.

On the other hand, ask yourself if you are being too picky and unable to make certain compromises. The excuse of not being able to find adequate child care often comes from women who feel guilty about leaving a child or who do not want to work in the first place. This is the perfect excuse to stay home. Examine your motives. Why are you returning to work? Are your parents, friends or relatives criticizing you? Do you feel badly about leaving your child because of your own childhood? Do you feel threatened by the fact that someone else will be caring for your child most of the day—perhaps better than you? Do you feel that your child may love that person more?

It is best to resolve these conflicts prior to going to work. Your child can sense an anxious parent and become anxious. An older child can attempt to manipulate the situation by complaining about the caretaker and begging you to stay home. This can shake up any mother who is not resolute about what she wants. You must feel secure within yourself about your decisions. Once you feel secure, you can make some compromises in your child-care requirements.

Q. *The other day when I went to pick up my child she called the caretaker "mommy" by accident. How should I feel about this?*

A. Don't let this upset you. Be happy that she has developed a warm and loving relationship with the caretaker. This is a sign of psychological health. Children should be able to form a number of relationships. Each good relationship and each positive experience will help to build her self-esteem and socialization skills. In many foreign countries there are several adults caring for a child—aunts, mothers, grandmothers—and the child can form a good relationship with each one. Studies have shown that despite child-care arrangements, mother and father remain the primary people in children's lives.

Q. *What if my caretaker asks me to lend her money or asks for advance payment?*

A. Ask yourself the following questions:

1. How long has she been my employee? Has she been hard working, honest, reliable?

2. How much money can I afford to lose, if for some reason she never pays me back?

Our main suggestion is not to become involved in the savings and loan industry. If, however, you have a soft heart and a loyal employee, here are some guidelines:

1. Only lend money or pay in advance to an employee that has been with you for at least six months.

2. Do not lend more than you can afford to lose. Our maximum is $100.

3. Only give one loan or advance at a time. Do not give any more until the first loan is paid off.

4. Agree on a payback schedule with your employee (usually through paycheck deductions). Write out the payback schedule and tack it onto the refrigerator with the dates and amounts to be paid back. Check off each amount as it is paid back (if it is a day-care mother, make sure you both have the schedule and you both check off payback).

Q. *When should I give my caretaker a raise? And how much?*

A. If she is doing a good job, don't wait until she asks you. A good rule of thumb is a year. How much depends on how much you can afford. (We should point out that day-care mothers usually have set fees, so you will have to go along with her fees.) How much are other people paying? Is her current salary adequate for the work that she does (in comparison to others in the community)? Have you added new responsibilities? How much was *your* raise this year? A good rule may be between 4 and 8 percent, depending on the above. Remember also to give her a Christmas bonus. Cash always comes in handy.

Q. *My caretaker's work has not been up to par. How do I tactfully tell her?*

A. Give your caretaker a chance, but don't let the situation ride. She will not know that you are displeased if you do not tell her. Discuss the issues. "Jane, I like the way you take care of the children, but I think the house is getting messy. Are you having a difficult time organizing your work schedule?" "Mary, I think the baby's nap is too long. (Mary enjoys soap operas.) I want her awakened by 3 P.M., and I want you to take her outside every afternoon." To the day care mother, "I would prefer that my child not nap since she stays awake too late at night."

You may or may not be able to work these issues out to your satisfaction, and you may have to make compromises. The day-care mother may want to nap all the children at the same time to give herself a break. If she's good, then you may have to give in and let your child go to sleep later at night. You must be the judge. Above all, rank your needs. Are the most important ones being met? Can you make compromises on the less important ones?

Q. *How do I go about dismissing a caretaker?*

A. This is a very sensitive issue. With a day-care mother, it's easier; you do not take your child to her home anymore. With a day woman or live-in, it can be a more uncomfortable situation. Issues where health or safety have been jeopardized such as leaving a child in the tub to answer the phone or burning a hole in a pot on the stove, call for immediate dismissal.

Remember, you are the employer, it's your child and your money, and your important needs have to be met. However, when dismissing someone, try to keep her ego intact. "Martha, you did an excellent job of caring for the baby, but I know it was difficult for you to handle my three-year-old. I must look for someone who can handle both children." "Jeanette, I know you were busy with the children and forgot about the stove, but it was a dangerous situation. I need to find someone who can handle the children and household management more efficiently."

Don't hesitate to dismiss someone because you don't want to go through the hassle of finding someone else. The best of all possible worlds, of course, is to find someone else prior to dismissing your current employee.

Q. *How much notice should I give when I dismiss someone?*

A. If you think your child is getting poor care, then that caretaker should be dismissed immediately. You want to avoid tension in your home if you have a live-in or day woman. If a pleasant atmosphere can be maintained with consistent care for the children, then a two-week notice is appropriate.

Q. *Should I give severance pay?*

A. We advise that your caretaker work for at least six months before receiving severance pay. (A day-care mother may have other stipulations.) Depending on the kind of job she did and your relationship, it may be appropriate to give one- to two-weeks severance pay. If you deducted unemployment benefits from her paycheck, then she is entitled to collect unemployment.

Q. *My day care mother is beginning to toilet train my 20 month old. I think this is too young, but she says it's not. What should I do?*

A. Much depends on the muscle capability of your child and her method of training. If your child sees older toilet trained children in day care, this can be peer stimulation to learn. On the other hand, your day care mother could be the one who is trained (putting your child on the toilet at the proper time) rather than your child. What is her attitude? Is your child punished for an "accident"? How does your child respond when you put her on the toilet at home?

This may be a situation representing a power struggle between you and the day care mother. If you feel this is adversely affecting your child, you may have to remove her from the day care situation. However if your child seems to be generally happy at day care and at home, maintain status quo and watch your child closely.

Toilet training is just one example of many issues that will arise which you will need to work out with the day care mother. Others may be training to use utensils, napping, eating solids, and discipline.

Q. *My day care mother allows the children to walk around the house with food in their hand. We have a rule in our home about keeping food in the kitchen. How will this inconsistency affect my child?*

A. Many parents worry about inconsistencies between their home and the home of the day care mother. While it would be ideal to have everything consistent, this is not reality. With reinforcement, however, a child can soon learn to distinguish what he can do at the caretaker's house and what he is allowed to do at home. An older child may even test you, telling you that Mrs. Doe lets him do certain things at her house. Stick to your guns. He will understand the rules.

*   *   *   *

Nursery Schools and Day Care Centers

When your child is between the ages of two and three, it is time to consider putting him or her in a more social environment that can also offer equipment that is not available either at home or the home of a day-care mother.

HINT: Begin examining day-care centers and nursery schools in the late winter or early spring for fall entry. Some centers and schools are so crowded you may have to register a year in advance. Don't be caught short at the last minute.

We think selecting a day-care center or nursery school is much easier than finding a single caretaker for your child. With centers and nursery schools, it is easier to observe the staff and environment and form your own impressions. You don't have to worry as much about the hidden idiosyncracies of a single caretaker. So take heart!

Your child has now grown and has different needs. The need for an intense one-to-one interaction has decreased somewhat. Your child is ready for further socialization. It is a most exciting time for children. They are discovering the world. Their minds are like sponges soaking in new information, and they delight in learning. You are selecting an environment that your child will be happy and thrive in, and a staff that will build on the child's esteem and give social and emotional developmental opportunities.

Important Features

The first thing to decide is what kind of atmosphere you want. Would your child do better in a more structured situation, a *laissez-faire* environment, or a mixture? Do you want an emphasis on art and music, or an emphasis on reading readiness? If you have a child with special needs or have qualms about your ability to match your child's needs to the right nursery school or center, we strongly suggest that you take the extra time to meet with the directors and a sample of teachers to discuss your concerns and their philosophies.

Other factors are: How much can you afford? What is located near your house or workplace? Which schools have hours that can accommodate your work schedule? Be sure to examine the school's vacation calendar. Some schools close for the summer, some have summer programs. List those factors that you think will be necessities, such as operating hours, or environmental priorities.

Word of mouth is most important. Check with friends first, then check with the agencies in your area that license nursery schools or day-care centers. Try health departments, offices for children, boards of education, and consult your local library for a list of licensed facilities. Telephone screen first. See Chart 7 (page 41). Then make an appointment to observe, and if possible, talk with the teacher and director.

The Visit

Visiting a nursery school or day-care center can be overwhelming. There is a lot to observe. It is helpful to bring along a checklist.   We have provided you with a checklist (Chart 8, page 43) focusing on four areas: (1) requirements and necessities, such as proper licensing and basic curricula; (2) activities and equipment, such as healthy snacks, routine schedules; (3) children, their behavior and how they are handled; (4) staff. Take this checklist to each center or school that you visit.

Making Your Decision

We're compulsive and need even more than a checklist to assist us. What follows is a simple, objective guide for rating the programs that you visit on factors that are important to you.

In the example, we chose staff as most important in schools and centers. We all know the influence that teachers and aides can have in building a child's self-esteem and in the development of socialization skills. Moreover, most of your interaction with the school or center will be with the staff. Does the facility have an environment where free and easy communication between staff members and parents is in evidence? Are staff experienced? Is there a history of low turnover? Are staff interacting in a positive fashion

(continued on page 47)

CHART 7: How to Conduct a Telephone Screening Interview With Nursery School/Day Care Center

Name of school/center _____

Address _____

Phone _____

Director _____

1. What age children do you take?

2. What are the number of children in your program?

   In each class?   How many classes?

3. What are your hours of operation?

4. Is transportation available?

5. Are breakfasts, lunches, or snacks provided?

6. Are you open in summer?   Vacations?

7. Is toilet training required?

8. What is the ratio of children to teacher?   Teacher aides?

9. What is your philosophy/emphasis of school/center, e.g., reading readiness, art?

10. What are your fees?

11. Can you accommodate children with special needs? (handicap, or medication)

12. Ask for a brochure.

Impressions:

CHART 8: Evaluation Checklist for Visiting Schools and Day-Care Centers

Check for the following	Yes	No	Not applicable	Notes
1. **Requirements and Necessities** a. Licensed by county and/or state.				
b. Number and ages of children (staff/ student ratio) follow county or state regulations.				
c. Staff are well qualified in education and/ or experience.				
d. Policy of school/center is in writing, e.g., opening and closing hours, snow and holidays, parent and center responsibility in event of illness or accident, insurance, payment of fees, adjustment for absenteeism, notice of withdrawal, giving medication, parent participation in the exchange of information between staff and parents, health requirements for children, visiting policies				
e. Five basic curriculum areas are covered: (1) housekeeping, (2) library, (3) block area, (4) art, (5) puzzles, table games. These are suggested. Additional areas include: water play, sandbox, carpentry, science, animals and plants, large muscle activities, music, language, numbers, social studies.				
f. Environment pleasant—lots of light, bright colors, things to look at.				
g. Material is at eye-level for children, it is out where they can see it.				
h. Meals and snacks are healthy and readily available.				

Check for the following	Yes	No	Not applicable	Notes
2. Activities and Equipment i. Mix of individual and group activities is in evidence.				
j. Key episodes (arriving and departing, naptime, mealtimes) or transitions are orderly.				
k. There is emphasis on continuity; there is flexibility without rigid programming schedule. Yet a routine or normal schedule is in evidence.				
l. Indoor and outdoor facilities and equipment for gross and fine motor development are in good repair, safe, readily available.				

CHART 8: Evaluation Checklist for Visiting Schools and Day-Care Centers (continued)

Check for the followin	Yes	No	Not applicable	Notes
3. **Children** m. Reaction/behavior of children is positive.				
n. Social and emotional developmental opportunities, e.g., considering rights of other children, sharing, standing up for own rights when necessary, are encouraged and modeled.				
o. Children make their own projects, e.g., creativity and problem-solving are emphasized.				
p. Activities are nonsexist.				
q. Children are grouped by age and/or they are mixed (there is no right or wrong way, it depends on your philosophy, particular activities).				
r. Center/school helps children develop wholesome attitudes towards their own bodies and bodily functions, e.g., physical differences between boys and girls handled matter-of-factly, toileting and undressing handled casually, handicaps, illnesses accepted in honest, open manner.				

CHART 8: Evaluation Checklist for Visiting Schools and Day-Care Centers (continued)

Check for the following	Yes	No	Not applicable	Notes
4. Staff s. Philosophy: teamwork between parents and caretaker or staff are to your liking.				
t. Parental involvement is encouraged.				
u. Conferences with teacher/child-care worker are regularly scheduled.				
v. Teachers use the aides in a positive, efficient manner; the teacher is able to delegate responsibility to the aide, there is "warmth" between the two individuals in the classroom.				
w. Staff are not only academically qualified but seem to be psychologically astute and observant of behavioral problems. Disciplinary techniques are to your liking; staff seems nonjudgmental and "blame" is not the first reaction to an incident.				
x. Staff stress accomplishments and progress.				
y. Division of tasks among staff is orderly and consistent.				

(continued from page 40)

with the child? We also emphasize the importance of the teacher's aide and how she is used as a staff member. She should not be a "go-fer," pouring juice and cleaning the room. She should take an active part and have an active relationship with the children under the supervision of the teacher. An aide can be as influential with your child as the teacher.

Past problems with day-care centers revolved around the issues of numerous caretakers, lack of opportunities, and insufficient continuity. Pay particular attention to:

- Consistency: same staff assigned to same group of children
- Opportunity: to practice different developmental skills
- Continuity: setting, schedule, staff, and other children all remain the same

Follow the "Guide to Chart 9" (page 49). Remember, use your own ideas to decide important factors in a school or center.

Questions and Answers on Nursery Schools and Day-Care Centers

Q. *Eight a.m. until 6 p.m. is a long day for a young child in an "institutional environment," no matter how pleasant. Is it possible to have my child attend a nursery school or day-care center for half the day and then come home or go to a day-care mother for the other half of the day?*

A. Yes, this is possible. Many parents feel that the school day is too long for a young child even though nap time is included (in some cases cots and a separate sleeping area are mandatory under licensing requirements). They feel their child needs time to wind down in the afternoon and will often need more individual attention.

But there are some problems. Either you will have to leave your job at midday to transport your child or you will have to arrange a carpool, where you will drive in the morning and someone else picks up the child in the afternoon (usually around noontime). If your carpool mate is ill, who will pick up? Or if the nursery school provides bus service, you will probably have to pay extra for it. Check your pocketbook. What can you afford? The addition of a day-care mother or housekeeper will probably add more to your costs than the reduction in cost from less time in school or center. However, if your house-

(continued on page 55)

CHART 9A: Guide for Selecting School or Day-Care Center

You have narrowed your list of choices to four. Judge these schools or centers according to factors most important to you. These might include: health, environment and space, equipment, language development, staff, parental involvement, staff-student interaction, location, cost, general impression. Using Chart 9C, you can either make brief notes in each box as you visit the schools or centers, <u>or</u> you can follow these steps:

STEP <u>A</u>: *Weight* each factor. For example, if staff is of greatest importance to you, give staff a weight of 9.

Example:
general impression (least important)	1
cost	2
location	3
health, enviroment, space	4
parental involvement	5
equipment	6
language development	7
interaction	8
staff (most important)	9

STEP <u>B</u>: *Rate* each school or center according to each factor on a 1–5 scale (1 = lowest; 5 = highest). For example, if school #1 rates high in staff, assign that school a 5.

Example:
general impression	1
cost	3
location	5
health, environment, space	4
parental involvement	1
equipment	2
language development	3
interaction	4
staff (most important)	5

STEP C: After you have assigned each school or center a rating for each weighted factor, multiply the weight times the rate for each box on the chart. For example, School #1 rating for staff (5) × weighting for staff (9) = 45.

Example: B   A   B × A = C

School #1 Rate × Weight =

general impression........................... 1 × 1 = 1

cost .... 3 × 2 = 6

location .... 5 × 3 = 15

health/environment/space .... 4 × 4 = 16

parental involvement .... 1 × 5 = 5

equipment................................. 2 × 6 = 12

language development .... 3 × 7 = 21

interaction................................ 4 × 8 = 32

staff (most important) .... 5 × 9 = 45

STEP D: Achieve a final "score" (D) for each school or center by adding each of the multiplied figures (C) for each school or center. For example, your score for School #1 is *153*.

Example:

School #1

$$\frac{C}{1} + \frac{C}{6} \ldots + 15 + 16 + 5 + 12 + 21 + 32 + 45 + \quad = \frac{D}{153}$$

STEP E: Compare scores on four schools. *Highest score* will come closest to what *you desire* in a school or day-care center

CHART 9B: Selection of School or Day-Care Center (Sample)

Day Care Center/School	Health, environment, Space (4)	Equipment (6)	Language Development (7)	Staff (9)	Parental Involvement (5)	Staff-student interaction (8)
1	Separate napping space, well-lighted (4)	Average (2)	No field trips; one-to-one conversations, circle time (3)	Low turnover; enthusiastic, warm (5)	No formal opportunity (1)	Small group interaction, some one-on-one activities (4)
2	Private outdoor play area, large indoor	New blocks; manipulative toys, wide varietiy	Very little one-on-one conversation with students	Low turn over, ok	Parental meetings with staff twice per year	Average
3	Outdoor space small	Sandbox and old toys	Reading group; circle time	Seem warm; lots of hugs; several new teachers	Informal, encouraged	Lots of one-on-one and organized group work
4	Seems adequate	Books, plants, animals, water toys	Lots of small group discussions	High turnover; 1 good, 1 adequate teacher	Vague	Lots of small groups, no one-on-one

CHART 9B: Selection of School or Day-Care Center (Sample) (continued)

Day Care Center/School	Location (3)	Cost (2)	General impression (1)	Philosophy	References, recommendations
				Additional Notes	
1	5-minute drive (5)	Average (3)	Negative (1)	Very structured; learning emphasized	Two good references
2	Half-hour drive	Average	Positive	Some structure; some freedom; emphasis on socialization	None
3	Possible carpool, 10 minutes	Costly	Neutral	Very structured and academic	1 good 1 bad
4	10-minute drive	Less costly	Neutral	Unstructured loose, not much academics	1 bad

CHART 9C: Selection of School or Day-Care Center

Day Care Center/School	Health, environment, space	Equipment	Language development	Staff	Parental involvement	Staff/student interaction
1						
2						
3						
4						

CHART 9C: Selection of School or Day-Care Center (continued)

Day Care Center/School	Location	Cost	General impression	Philosophy	References, recommendations
				Additional Notes	
1					
2					
3					
4					

(continued from page 47)

keeper is currently caring for an infant at home, having your three-year-old come home in the afternoon could be less costly.

Rebecca has had both of her children in nursery school all day. She feels they are better off remaining in one place and she has less to deal with logistically. She is also a firm believer in organized play and peer stimulation. Michele has chosen a half-day nursery school with her children coming home to a day woman. She feels it is necessary for her children to unwind and to get more individual attention. She drives the car pool in the mornings, but her work is close to home and school so that she could pick up at noon if her car-pool mate could not. The above arrangements have worked out well for both of us.

Q. *How do I prepare my child for the transition from housekeeper or day-care mother to a nursery school or day-care center?*

A. This is an important question and requires thought and care. This transition may be somewhat easier for children who have been with a day-care mother because they're used to sharing the day with other children. For children who have been alone with a housekeeper, the change may be more difficult. Any preparation you can give a child is helpful. One suggestion is a play group for your child which your caretaker could join. A play group usually meets once-a-week, for two hours, and is run by mothers for their toddlers. The basic purpose is socialization.

Some other ideas are:

- Take a few hours off from work (or a Saturday) and take your child to some of the parent-child classes that your county offers (toddler gym, music, art, for example). This will provide the experience with other children.

- Make up a storybook (see sample) with either pictures you have drawn or cut from a magazine, about your child going to school. Sequential pictures can illustrate a school day, starting with saying good-bye to mommy or daddy, the car-pool trip, playing at school and having fun, eating snacks at school, greeting the parent at pick-up time, and supper at home. It is important to depict the scenes of the morning good-bye, and the afternoon pick-up. That way, your child knows you are coming back! Go over the book pictures with the child and let him or her ask

Storybook

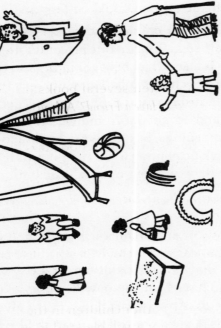

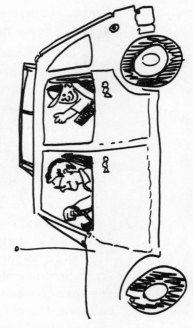

Arriving at school or center

Driving home

Saying goodbye to the day-care mother

Time to go home

questions. It is an important item to be taken to school on the first day. If your child is negative about the book in the beginning, don't be concerned. Your child knows change is coming, and this negativeness is a way of dealing with change for the moment.

- Check out books from the library dealing with the school situation. Miriam Cohen has written several books on this subject, including our favorite: *Will I Have a Friend?* Ask your librarian for other suggestions.

- The week before your child is to begin school, take him or her to the school in the late afternoon and stay there with your child for about one hour. Most schools have unstructured time in the afternoon, so you would not be interfering—though it is a good idea to check with the teachers first. They may have additional suggestions. If you cannot take off from work to do this, perhaps you can arrange for someone else to help you. If not, take your child to the school playground on your time off. Let your child see the school building and play on the outside equipment.

- Try to find out the names of other children in the class. Call the registrar. A class list is usually available (and is also helpful for arranging car pools). Do this at least two weeks before the start of school so your child can meet some of the children prior to beginning school.

- The first day of school walk in with your child and try to interest him or her in some of the toys. Stay about 10 minutes (ask the teacher's judgment on this). Then give a firm kiss, assure your child you will be back at a specific time and leave. If your child begins to cry, the teacher should take over.

Q. *Several of my neighbors send their children to a close by nursery school. My child is two years old, and I am ready to register him for school next September. Should I accept their recommendations (and carpool) and send my child to the same school? I feel guilty about relying on their choices without doing some homework myself.*

A. Don't rely on their recommendation. It will be wonderful if, after you have observed a few schools, you choose the same program for your child. There are lots of good reasons for sending your child to the same school such as convenience for you and more immediate friendships and easier transition for your child. These criteria should be given weight in your final decision of a school.

However, you must pay primary attention to your child's individual needs. This school may or may not meet these needs. Also, minor problems will arise at any school. If you have knowledge of the positives and negatives of other schools, you can more readily identify and accept problems and deal with them. If you have not taken the time to educate yourself about nursery schools and day care centers, you will be operating in a vacuum.

Q. *My husband does not want to send our three and a half year old daughter to a day care center. He pictures a cold environment, with no warmth from caretakers, and no emphasis on learning. He prefers that our child remain with her day-care mother, until she is kindergarten age. I have a mixed opinion. What should we do?*

A. There is no right or wrong to this. There is no magic age for transitioning to a school or center. We have a few hints to help you in your decision:

- Be sure that your day-care mother is providing stimulating toys and games to your child. It is even better if she cares for other children of your child's age.

- Have your husband arrange to visit a few day-care centers and discuss his concerns with a director and a few teachers. His opinion may be based on some "horror stories" about day-care centers from years ago.

- Both of you should bring your child to one or two centers that you have preselected and observe her reaction. Is she enthused? Or frightened by the noise and activity? Encourage your child to join in, and observe her response to the other children and the caretaker.

- Don't be too hasty to sever relations with your day care mother. Explain to her what you are doing and agree on a fair termination date if that is decided.

Monitoring and Prevention

You have a nonverbal infant. You have a verbal imaginative youngster. You will ask "How do I know if my children are happy? How do I know if they are well taken care of?" The most important part of child care is the part people usually pay the least attention to: monitoring. Remember, children, parents, jobs, caretakers, and school situations *change*. Initiating a change when things seem to be going smoothly is particularly difficult. We would prefer to close our eyes to some things and not "rock the boat." We urge you to keep ahead of the game, and you will save yourself time, energy, and lots of aggravation. Prevention and monitoring go hand-in-hand. By proper monitoring you can prevent numerous problems inherent to child-care.

Monitoring is a continuous process. One must continually stop, think, discuss, and reevaluate. When you discuss a situation with your child's caretaker or teacher, probe. Ask questions. When you need to reevaluate, send others to observe for you before making a final decision. For instance, your verbal youngster's complaints about the housekeeper could stem from a variety of reasons ranging from boredom to the housekeeper's actual neglect. You need more information before making a decision.

On Chart 10 (page 61) you will find questions to ask yourself about your child-care arrangements. Remember though, many of these questions call for judgments, not definite answers. But if there is something about the caretaker or school that is bothering you—however undefined the problem—don't let it linger. Try to make appropriate changes, then keep your eye on things more closely and wait for improvement. Chart 11 (page 62) reviews potential problem areas.

Try to take five minutes at the end of each day to discuss your child's day with the caretaker. However, this is not always feasible. At a minimum you should have a weekly discussion with your caretaker. In the interim, ask her to fill out an activities chart for your child (Chart 12A, page 63). It is a good way to know what is happening with your nonverbal infant or toddler during a day with the caretaker. It should only take one minute to fill out the chart. Remember, this should *not* substitute for your weekly discussion time with your caretaker.

Monitoring Questions and Answers

Q. *I fear my child might come to physical harm under the supervision of the caretaker. If this happened I could never forgive myself. How can I get rid of this guilt feeling? Should I trust the caretaker to adequately care for my child?*

A. One of the worst fears of parents is that their children could come to harm under the supervision of a caretaker. This can be a normal concern when you are leaving your child for the first time. Toddlers learning to walk and explore are prone to accidents. But try to realize that these accidents can happen in your presence as well. Rebecca's older son took a flying leap off the couch, and split his lip, right in front of her eyes. Soon after, her younger son fell out of the crib at grandma's house. Then he broke his arm on the monkey bars at camp.

You can make judgments about your caretaker's safety consciousness by observation. You can child-proof your house and make sure that the day-care mother's house is also child-proof. Frequent visits at odd intervals are helpful here, too. But you must realize that you cannot control everything.

Q. *My child complained that the caretaker gave him a spanking. Should I allow the caretaker to punish my child?*

A. The area of discipline should be discussed with your caretaker when you are first interviewing her. If she believes in spanking and you don't, is she willing to listen to your wishes? What kind of punishment does she use? What kinds of situations would she punish a child for?

Your child should have only age-appropriate discipline and should also be disciplined immediately after an inappropriate action. If your child runs into the street, this needs to be dealt with immediately. The child might not remember this action if the caretaker has to wait for you to come home. A firm no and a few taps on the hand or the bottom, or sitting in the corner are sometimes needed to help a child build inner controls and understand right from wrong.

Find out from your caretaker what your child did to deserve the spanking. Is it something you would have punished him for if you had been there? If so, support your caretaker and let your child know you agree with her actions. If not, discuss the situation with the caretaker privately.

(continued on page 65)

CHART 10: Monitoring Child Care

What do you look for once your child is already in care?

- Does the child cry on the way to the caretaker, and/or after you leave? How long?
- Anything out of the ordinary that lasts more than a month or two in a new situation should be examined. Crying? Bring to attention of teacher, caretaker.
- How does the child greet you when you arrive?
- What are the child's habits like at home? Overly cranky or irritable? Does the child eat and sleep well?
- How does he compare in terms of development with other children his age? Is he within a "normal range"?
- For a baby—is baby clean and neat? Have bowel movements been taken care of?
- What does the verbal child say about her experiences? What indirect signs do you detect from her experiences? (Does she sing a new song or do something new?)
- Has caretaker dropped hints or complained?
- Have there been any major schedule changes (yours, caretaker's or school's)?
- Is there anything happening in caretaker's or teacher's life that may affect child-care functioning, for example, divorce, illness?
- Do you detect a change in household standards of your caretaker? Your day-care mother? In school or center?
- Do you have regular teacher conferences?

HINTS:

- Children go through stages; for example, eight months to 15 months is particularly known for separation anxiety.
- When child begins to verbalize, you must sort out what is real and what is imaginary.
- Drop in unexpectedly as often as you can.

CHART 11: Problem Prevention

DO YOU . . .

- Discuss child's habits, likes and dislikes with caretaker/teacher? How often?

- Pay on time, arrive on time, offer gifts or bonuses, extra days off?

- Make surprise visits; overlap with caretaker periodically?

- Have a neighbor or relative drop in unexpectedly?

- Prepare written agreement of expectations between caretaker and parents?

- Review this agreement with caretaker at regular intervals?

- Prepare child for changes or transitions, such as caretaker to nursery school, different caretakers, schedule changes?

- Discuss the day with your toddler in a relaxed manner?

- Let your caretaker know immediately when something she does is not satisfactory rather than keeping it to yourself and letting tension build?

- Compare notes with other parents who use the same caretaker or school?

- Compare notes with parents using a different caretaker or school?

CHART 12A: Activities (Sample)

Breakfast	7:30 a.m. (good)
Lunch	11:30 a.m. (light)
Snack	none
Bath	before p.m. nap
Walk/Outdoor play	after nap
Bowel movements (if infant)	one — p.m.
Fussy day	no
Calm day	yes
Games, entertainment	peek-a-boo, books, puzzles, crawling outside
Special events	waved "bye-bye" learned new song

CHART 12B: Activities

Breakfast

Lunch

Snack

Bath

Walk/Outdoor play

Bowel movements

Fussy day

Calm day

Games, entertainment

Special events

HINT: Make copies of this chart and ask your caretaker to record your child's daily schedule.

(continued from page 60)

Q. *My four-year-old child told me that the caretaker wouldn't play with her all day. How do I determine the truth to this?*

A. It is indeed sometimes difficult to determine what is real and what is exaggeration—particularly with an imaginative four-year-old. Your caretaker could have played with your child most of the day, and your child may be complaining about the one hour that she did housework. Does your child complain often? If so, it may mean that she is bored and would enjoy a day-care center or nursery school (or extended hours if she is already attending school). On the other hand, if your child complains often, it could be that the chemistry between your housekeeper and child is not right. It is also possible, of course, that your housekeeper is watching television all day. Ask your housekeeper how a typical day is spent. You should suggest specific things for your child and housekeeper to do together such as baking brownies, a walk to the park, or a specific game to play. A friend of Michele's prepared a box of craft activities for each week. This extra effort put her mind at ease, gave her child some extra stimulation and gave the caretaker a clear message of her expectations. Tell her that your child seems dissatisfied and ask *her* for suggestions for improving the situation. Make some surprise visits—or send a neighbor or friend.

Q. *My child clings and cries desperately when I leave him at the caretaker/school. I get reports that he is happy during the day. What can I do?*

A. How old is your child? If between eight and 15 months, your child is probably suffering from separation anxiety, a natural occurrence among children at that age. It will probably pass once your child feels secure with the knowledge that you will return. The key is the report from the caretaker that your child is happy and doing well during the day.

How long does the crying last after you have gone? Anything under 15 minutes should be discounted. If you can stay unnoticed a few minutes and observe your child, you'll feel that much better if you can see your child happily playing. How is he at home? Does he cling to you around the house? Does he go out and play with other children without hesitation? Does he seem happy and generally content?

If the problem appears to be mainly separating from you in the morning, then we suggest some behavior modification, if your child is old enough to understand. Try this: Get a calendar and some sticky stars or draw a happy face. Each day that he does not cry he will get a happy face on his calendar and a surprise. (This could be something simple like an ice cream cone or a small toy.) If he cries, then no surprise and no happy face. This may help to extinguish some of this unhappy behavior.

Q. *My child stayed with a caretaker in my home until he was two and a half. This year he is attending a morning nursery school. The first two weeks went beautifully. Now he is crying, resisting his teacher and misbehaving at school. Is it the teacher? the school? Should I pull him out and return to full-time in-home care?*

A. Your child has recognized a major change in his lifestyle, at a very difficult stage in his life. He is used to individual attention at home, and now (after the novelty of a new situation has worn off) is trying to adjust to a new schedule, new authority figures, and new children. Above all, be patient. Don't pull him out of school unless you are certain that it is the wrong school for him. He needs to know that school will be part of his life, and having a tantrum won't change that. Talk to the teacher and aide in private. Suggest that they spend some special time with him. The teacher could make him her special helper, for instance, by asking him to pass out crayons, or cups for juice. He needs some extra attention just now. Allow him to take something from home with him to school: a favorite stuffed animal or toy. (We know plenty of happy, adjusted children who still carry their blankets to school in their big boy/girl bookbags)! Also, try some of the behavior modification techniques, as suggested in the previous answer.

Most important, don't allow him to see your anxiety or doubts. Tell him you are dropping him off at school, you are going to work, and that you will be home to play with him later. Then give him a big hug and kiss at the door, and turn around and walk out, without looking back. If this behavior continues, have another conference with the teacher and director, and consider a more major change.

Q. *The day-care center my daughter attends experienced an increase in staff turnover this year. Should I be concerned?*

A. Yes. The stability of the staff is a key factor in any nursery school or day-care center. Seeing the same staff day after day brings a sense of security to your child. Your child also builds loving relationships with them. A high rate of turnover can be unsettling to young children.

It sounds like this school is suffering some internal problems. You should talk with the director or administrator of the school. Examine other aspects of the situation as well. Have the school physical facilities been maintained? Are there adequate materials for the children to use? Is there open communication between parents and staff? Has there been a decrease in parent meetings? You may need to decide whether you should consider a change in school next year.

Q. *My child is four years old and in nursery school. He is coming home with bad language. How can I control this?*

A. Wait till they enter elementary school! If we do not make too much of an issue out of it, the kids do not get thrills from saying the forbidden, and the bad language will diminish. You can also tell your child gently, but firmly, that language like that is not permitted in the house.

Perhaps you are concerned about the kinds of influences your child is being exposed to at nursery school. Talk with the teachers. Have they heard the language? How have they handled the situation? Ask yourself if the atmosphere in the school is emotionally healthy for your child. If you think your child is generally happy in the situation, don't worry. Most likely, the language problem will go away.

Q. *My child is 15 months old and not walking. Should I worry? Maybe the caretaker isn't giving my child enough opportunities to learn. What should I do?*

A. Don't panic. There are many children who walk late. To assure yourself, however, you should have your child checked by a pediatrician. If all is physically well, talk to your caretaker. Discourage her from carrying your child all the time. Does your caretaker go to get something for your child rather than letting her try to get it herself? Encourage her to walk *with* your child to retrieve things. How long does your child spend in the crib? Does she interact with other children near her age who are walking and could be role models? A play group could also help.

Q. *My baby doesn't go to sleep until late at night after a long day. What does this mean?*

A. Is your baby grumpy at night? Irritable or overtired in the morning? Most likely, your baby is napping too long in the afternoon. Check with the caretaker. Maybe you and the caretaker need to rearrange the schedule. Shorten nap hours and see what happens. If the answers to all of the above questions are no, then it just might mean that your baby is not a sleeper and has more stamina than you do!

Q. *My day-care mother mentioned casually that her husband is retiring. Should I pursue this?*

A. Certainly. You have a right to know what her plans will be after her husband retires. Will she continue to be a day-care mother or will they be moving to Florida? She may be afraid to tell you her plans for fear that you will make alternative arrangements immediately, thereby decreasing her paycheck. Let her know that you want to work together with her in anticipating and making future changes needed for your child.

Q. *The house has not been as clean as it should be. My housekeeper says the baby is getting more demanding. What should I do?*

A. How old is your child? If your child is reaching the toddler stage, this active being is probably keeping the housekeeper busy. If your child is older she or he may be demanding that the caretaker play all the time. This could indicate that the child is ready for a nursery school situation. Ask your housekeeper how the day is usually spent. Perhaps you need to change your expectations of how much housework can be done with an active toddler in tow. Use the Change Chart in Section II and discuss changes with the housekeeper. See if things get better with some revisions in the work schedule.

On the other hand you might be suspicious that your housekeeper is watching soap operas instead of doing housework. You could make some surprise visits home to find out or have a neighbor come by to borrow sugar. Keep your eye on the situation.

Q. *Lately, my housekeeper has indicated that she must leave early. She offers no explanations. I hate to probe into her personal affairs, but I am worried that she is losing interest in the job. What should I do?*

A. Your housekeeper could have a number of reasons for leaving early, ranging from physical problems to job hunting! Schedule a discussion time with her. She may or may not choose to divulge her whereabouts. However, encourage her to discuss any problems or raise questions about your requirements and her responsibilities. If there are difficulties in your relationship which might be motivating her to seek a job elsewhere, this is the opportunity to identify them early and prevent bigger—perhaps unresolvable—problems. If she is ill, you should also know. She may need extended sick-leave in the future, and you will need to know in order to make backup arrangements.

Q. *I came home early the other day and found my housekeeper washing and drying her laundry in my washer and dryer. I pretended not to notice, but find that I resent this. How should I handle this?*

A. You don't want to ignore the situation. Resentment can build, and you will soon find yourself noticing other problems and feeling dissatisfied. At worst, your children will feel the tension in the house and be uncomfortable. On the other hand, don't overreact and criticize or ask for explanations. Your caretaker may have done this in a past job with her former employer's blessing. Again, schedule a discussion time and raise this as one of the "understandings" you want to reach.

SECTION II

Home Management

Here are helpful hints and worksheets on home and time management. Managing a home can be a full-time job. Your aim is to condense this job into the shortest time span possible. (See Chart 13, page 72.) This task is almost as formidable as finding good child care. We have found that like child care, the duties on the home front demand constant reevaluation and change.

Many of the books we have read tell you how you should clean woodwork and dust blinds. We take a managerial approach. Your goal must be to accomplish as much as possible with as little time and energy expended as possible, and still come out with a satisfactory product. In other words, think the words *management, organization,* and *efficiency* instead of the word *housework.*

If this sounds foreign to you, read on and try the worksheets.

Time Management

Time is your most precious commodity. Develop "time guides" in your head. A "time guide" means that you have "time" on your mind, either quite consciously or in your preconscious, as you go about your day. Many decisions and activities will revolve around your time guides. Below are some of the time guides that we carry around in our heads every day. It is important when faced with time-management decisions to consider all of these items and to put them in perspective depending upon your particular situation. Soon they will become second nature to you.

CHART 13: Time Management

Since time at work is ususally fixed, your focus should be to minimize home-management time in order to maximize family, personal, and social time.

FIXED

Work Time

Specifically
scheduled

NEED TO MINIMIZE

Home Management Time*

Routine chores
Extra chores
Family management
Paper management

NEED TO MAXIMIZE

Family Time

Couple together

Couple with
children

Each spouse alone
with child

Personal Time

Personal goals

Leisure
activities

Socializing Time

Dating (singles)

Getting together
with friends

*Routine chores—cooking, cleaning, laundry
Extra chores—repairs, remodeling, changing seasonal clothes
Family management—doctor's/dentist appointments for kids, extracurricular
    activities, carpools
Paper management—bills, taxes, insurance

Time Guides

Time Value—How much do I value my time?

Forget how much money you make! On an hourly basis, how much do you value your time? How much money do you think your time is really worth? $5 an hour? $10? $25? $50 an hour? Use your "time value" as a guideline when making decisions about your time.

Your time value is $50 an hour. Is it worth it to go 15 minutes out of your way to save $5 on a sale item? That's $12.50 worth of your time! If you think your time is valued at $10 an hour, then it's $2.25 worth of your time! Half the savings on the sale item!

Ask yourself: How should I use my time now?

Make choices. Should I do the dishes now or should I sew a button on my shirt?

HINT: Divide chores into two categories:

1. Those that do not require much concentration—like dishes—and can be done when the children are awake.
2. Those that can be done better when children are asleep, like paper work and bill paying.

What will happen if it's not done today?

Will I need to wear the shirt in the next few days? If yes, I should sew the button on today.

My library books are overdue today. However, I will not be going in the direction of the library today. Should I wait a few days, pay the book fine, and combine the library trip with another close-by or should I go today and avoid a fine?

Which effort will give the best returns?

Look over the situation carefully. You can cut your efforts in half by planning carefully. A store specializing in sports equipment may be wasting time and money if it advertises to the general public. It is wiser to make special mailings to targeted people that belong to sports and health clubs, thereby cutting cost and increasing efficiency. You must do the same thing.

- Need to buy something special for your cousin's wedding? Don't pound the pavements and look in every shop. Use the Yellow Pages. Call a few specialty stores, ask for suggestions and prices. Pick out a gift and have them deliver.
- Your child has to go to the allergist once a week for shots. Don't beg your boss for extra leave. Pay someone to take him.
- Want a special book from the library? Call the library to learn if it's available; ask the librarian to put it on reserve and call you when it is available.
- Your house needs painting. Don't call 100 painters for estimates. Ask friends for recommendations and get estimates from three recommended painters.

Whose problem is it?

Your child is supposed to take some special arts and crafts material for school today. She forgets it. Should you leave work to bring the materials? Whose problem is it?

Your spouse's workroom is a mess. Whose problem is it?

Volunteer activities

When contemplating engaging in volunteer activities (clubs, other organizations) ask yourself:

- How many hours will this take?
- Will it help professional, business, social goals?
- How much is this effort worth? Will the compensation monetarily or otherwise (business contacts, self-satisfaction) be worth being away from my family?

Weekend rule

Household management duties should be minimized on weekends. Weekends are for personal and family time. Do not spend more than four hours during the weekend for household management.

Personal time

If you do not schedule personal time, you will not have it. Each spouse should have a fixed schedule for personal time—a minimum of five hours per week.

No matter how few hours are devoted to personal time, it will soften the "merry-go-round" feeling that hits us all.

Spending time with your child.

When you spend time with your child, ask yourself:
- *Will this activity contribute to my child's self-esteem?*
- *Will this activity enhance our relationship?*

A "yes" answer means quality time well spent.

Effective time management involves making immediate choices and time exchanges. If you take time out from work to attend your child's school picnic, this will contribute to the child's self-esteem and enhance your relationship. However, don't feel guilty if you work a few hours overtime on Saturday.

Putting "Management" in Your Home

Let's examine the meaning and styles of *home management,* keeping our time guides in mind. *To manage* means to have charge of, direct, conduct, administer. A *manager* is the person in overall charge. This person does not do all the work but streamlines the job, organizes it, and trains others to do it.

For example, you work 40 hours a week at the office. A new branch office is opening, and your boss gives you additional responsibility at the new branch without decreasing your current workload. What can you do? Do you double your work week to 80 hours? No! You reorganize without damaging the product. How?

- Consolidate: curtail phone interruptions and use specific time during the day to return calls.

- Delegate: train others to do some of the tasks you are currently doing.

- Innovate: find new ways of doing things—learn to speed read, use a dictaphone instead of writing out reports; purchase new time-saving equipment.

- Eliminate: put newsletter out biweekly instead of weekly.

There are many types of home management. Try to think of home management in terms of office management. (We know it's difficult to look at chocolate-covered hands on a wall in a professional manner.) But take a professional overview of the essentials that must be done in your home.

Types of Home Management

Below are four types of home management. There is some overlap between them. Look at them carefully. What kind of home management do you currently have? What would you like to change? What would be best for you?

Household Manager

One person is the household manager. The duties of a manager are to:
- examine all household tasks
- decide what needs to be done and how often, trying to routinize as much as possible
- delegate, through negotiation, particular areas of responsbility to: paid help, spouse, children, and self

With this system someone is "in charge" and has overall responsibility for a smooth household operation. Because one person has an overview, he or she can readily pinpoint problems in the system. However, the responsibility of "managing" puts an extra 5 to 10 percent burden on the "manager" in the dual-career couple. A trade-off in other areas could be made, for example, the manager gets more personal time or the manager does less housework.

Exclusive Domain

Each person may be exclusively responsible for certain home-management areas:
- husband in charge of everything pertaining to food: shopping, putting groceries away, menu planning, cooking, setting table, cleaning up, packing lunches.

- wife responsible for everything pertaining to clothes: deciding children's wardrobe needs, shopping, washing, folding, dry cleaning, alterations, ironing

Modified Version of Exclusive Domain

One person may have major responsibility for a particular area but may also delegate (through negotiation) minor responsibilities within that domain:

- husband (food chores): does cooking and grocery shopping but delegates cleaning up and setting table

Role Sharing

Role sharing simply means sharing and negotiating all household tasks. This makes it more difficult to fall into the "trap" of having someone do all. On the other hand, because there are several people involved, standards may be uneven and the "flow" of home management may not be quite as smooth.

We don't recommend one style of home management over the others. All involve negotiation between spouses. Answering the following questions may help you decide which method is best for your family:

- Does one spouse have exceptionally long hours or do a lot of traveling? If so, then the household manager approach may be better.
- What are the ages of your children? Small chores can be delegated to children as young as three.
- Is everyone willing to be flexible about household standards?
- Are there particular household chores that you absolutely detest?
- Are there particular chores that you can do particularly well?
- How much are you willing to pay for household help?

A good manager first tries to obtain a broad understanding of the current situation, then narrows the focus.

Consider the following key points when making changes.
- What overall needs to be done?
- What chores can be consolidated or eliminated?
- Look at chores that are done daily, weekly, monthly.

- Can daily tasks be changed to weekly? Can weeklies be changed to biweekly or monthly?
- What can be routinized?
- Who will do it?
- How well do you want it done?
- When will it be done?

SUGGESTION: The family member who does the chore sets the standard. If it is payment for service, you set the standard.

Change Chart

We favor using the Change Chart to help you in home management. First examine Chart 14 (page 79). This is a handy instrument to help you to determine where you and your family stand regarding home management. It should help you think about the kinds of changes you might like to make.

Then look at Chart 15 (page 80). It is especially geared to the family that decides on either the household manager, or the exclusive or modified domain. Even if you have a cleaning person, the chart will help you decide which chores you want done. Chart 15 serves as an example, using the category of food chores. All food chores are recorded on the chart. Under the "Current" heading you can see who does the chore, how often, and when. Under "Change," an effort was made to delegate, eliminate, and simplify. In our example, the wife previously did weekly food shopping. Now her husband will stock up on staples monthly while she buys perishables weekly. It will take 15 minutes of her time to buy perishables weekly and two hours of her husband's time to stock up, instead of the previous one and a half hours spent weekly by the wife. Also, the wife will become more organized through menu planning and will hire a mother's helper for the hectic dinner hours. This frees her up for more family time, and will probably result in better dinners.

The Change Chart is divided into seven categories. Examine these, and then add your own. What changes will help make the chores more manageable? Work on the chart with your family. Just reviewing the chores and current division of labor may lead to increased understanding about home roles and responsibilities.

CHART 14: Who Is Currently Responsible for Home Management?

Task	Husband Mostly	50/50	Wife mostly	Delegated third party. Who?
Grocery shopping				
Cooking				
Cleaning up after dinner				
Vacuuming				
Cleaning bathrooms				
Washing clothes				
Errand running, i.e., shoe repair, cleaner				
Gift buying for holidays and special occasions				
Shopping for children's clothes				
Taking child to doctors' appointments				
Staying home from work when child is sick				
Arranging day care or babysitter				
Making house repairs				
Maintaining car				

CHART 15: Change Chart (Sample)

Food Chores

Task	Current			Change			
	Who	*How often*	*When*	*Who (delegate)*	*How often (eliminate)*	*When (routinize)*	*Simplify, Modify*
Shopping	Wife	Weekly	Tuesday	Husband/ wife	Monthly/ weekly	Tuesday	Husband will stock up on staples monthly—wife will buy perishables weekly—time will be saved
Putting groceries away	Wife	Weekly	Tuesday	Children	Monthly/ weekly	Tuesday	
Meal planning	Wife	Daily		Wife	Weekly	Sunday	Wife will plan out menus on a weekly basis, instead of deciding last minute
Cooking	Wife	Daily		Wife/ mother's helper	Daily	Daily	Wife will cook in advance—mother's helper will heat up
Cleaning up after dinner	Wife	Daily		Husband/ children	Daily		
Packing lunches	Wife	Daily		Husband/ children	Daily		
Organizing kitchen	Wife	Monthly	Any day, no special time	Cleaning person	Bi-monthly	Friday	
Washing kitchen floor	Wife	Weekly		Cleaning person	Weekly	Friday	

CHART 15: Change Chart
Regular Home Maintenance

Task	Current			Change		
	Who	How often	When	Who (delegate)	How often (eliminate)	When (routinize)	Simplify, Modify
Dusting							
Wash kitchen floor							
Clean sinks, bathtubs, toilet bowls							
Clean stove							
Vacuum							
Wash woodwork, window sills							
Change linens, all beds							

Regular Home Maintenance (continued)

Task	Current			Change			
	Who	*How often*	*When*	*Who (delegate)*	*How often (eliminate)*	*When (routinize)*	*Simplify, Modify*
Clean refrigerator							
Sweep porch, sidewalk							
Remove clutter							
Wash windows							
Clean mirrors							
Water plants							
Empty garbage							

CHART 15: Change Chart (continued)

Extra Home Maintenance

Task	Current			Change		
	Who	How often	When	Who (delegate)	How often (eliminate)	When (routinize)	Simplify, Modify
Remodeling						
Decorating						
Appliance maintenance						
Lawn (cutting grass, gardening)						
House maintenance repairs						
Sorting children's toys and equipment to organize or dispose of						
Closet cleaning, storeroom cleaning						
Spring cleaning						

CHART 15: Change Chart (continued)
Food Chores

Task	Current			Change		
	Who	How often	When	Who (delegate)	How often (eliminate)	When (routinize)	Simplify, Modify

Task	Current			Change			
	Who	*How often*	*When*	*Who (delegate)*	*How often (eliminate)*	*When (routinize)*	*Simplify, Modify*
Shopping							
Putting groceries away							
Meal planning							
Cooking							
Setting table							
Cleaning up after dinner							
Doing dishes							
Packing lunches							
Straightening kitchen							
Sweeping kitchen floor							

CHART 15: Change Chart (continued)

Clothes Chores

Task	Current			Change		
	Who	How often	When	Who (delegate)	How often (eliminate)	When (routinize)	Simplify, Modify
Deciding children's wardrobe needs							
Shopping for children's clothes, shoes							
Washing							
Drying							
Folding							
Putting away							
Ironing							
Dry cleaning							
Alterations							
Changing seasonal clothes							
Straightening, organizing clothes, drawers, closets							

CHART 15: Change Chart (continued)
Money, Paper Management

Task	Current			Change		
	Who	How often	When	Who (delegate)	How often (eliminate)	When (routinize)	Simplify, Modify
Bills							
Insurance (health, life, home, and car)							
Taxes							
Stocks							
Bonds							
IRAs							
Installment purchases							
Investments							

CHART 15: Change Chart (continued)

Family Management

Task	Current			Change			
	Who	How often	When	Who (delegate)	How often (eliminate)	When (routinize)	Simplify, Modify
Finding and arranging child care							
Car pooling							
Attending school meetings							
Deciding with child on extracurricular activities (arranging schedule for those activities—infant swim, toddler gym, Suzuki violin, etc.)							
Helping with homework							
Giving children baths							
Arranging doctor and dentist appointments							
Picking up at day care or school if sick							
Getting baby sitters (nighttime)							

CHART 15: Change Chart (continued)

Family Management

Task	Current			Change			
	Who	How often	When	Who (delegate)	How often (eliminate)	When (routinize)	Simplify, Modify
Arranging playtime with other children							
Coordinating work schedules between spouses							
Making arrangements when children have school vacations							
Making arrangements for family vacations							
Gift and card buying for special occasions							
Planning business and personal entertainment obligation							
Care of pets							

CHART 15: Change Chart (continued)

Car Maintenance

Task	Current			Change			
	Who	How often	When	Who (delegate)	How often (eliminate)	When (routinize)	Simplify, Modify
Winterizing							
Tires							
General maintenance							
Car repair							
Car license, tags							

Like Scale

The following "Like" Scale is especially helpful if your family decides on the role-sharing managerial system. This scale helps you to figure out which tasks each family member should do based on what she or he likes to do best. The scale is based on a 1 to 10 continuum, (10, like best; 1 like least) and is excellent for avoiding, or reducing complaints and accusations of unfairness. A family meeting is the best time to fill out the scale. Children like to have a voice in family affairs and usually everyone is happier when they get what they choose. The family should have biweekly meetings to review the scale and negotiate changes. (It should be noted that if your children are too young to help out—below age three—the chart can be used by a couple, eliminating the children's columns or it can be used by a single parent, eliminating a spouse column.)

Estimates of the weekly number of hours a chore requires are also made to assure some equality. It is difficult, however, to reach perfect equality in home management. For various reasons such as work schedules, there may be a time imbalance. Also, it may not be expected that the children share equally with adults, but equally between themselves. The point is to divide chores as evenly as possible with some extra rewards for the person who might have more to do. Chart 16 (page 91) is a sample of the Like Scale.

CHART 16: "Like" Scale
(Sample)

Food chores	Wife	Husband	Child 1	Child 2	Estimated Hours weekly
Setting table	3	5	(8)	7	1 hour 10 minutes
Cooking	(8)	3	6	4	7 hours
Cleaning up	1	(4)	2	1	3½ hours
Grocery shopping	2	(6)	too young	too young	3 hours
Menu planning	4	6	8	(10)	10 minutes
Packing children's lunches	3	5	6	(8)	50 minutes

Time Balance

Wife	7 hours
Husband	6½ hours
Child 1	1 hour 10 minutes
Child 2	60 minutes

1. Make list of work to be done.
2. Use a 10-point scale, with 10 for the task you like best and 1 for the task you like least. Each person should rate the tasks according to likes and dislikes.
3. Estimate the number of hours weekly it will take to do the task.
4. The one with the highest "like" score on a particular task does it. (Circle the highest score in each category.)
5. List all tasks in all categories this way, i.e., house maintenance, clothes chores, etc. Then examine the estimated weekly hours combining all categories. Does one family member have many more weekly hours than the other?
6. If so, negotiate some tasks so there will not be a large "hour" imbalance—or you may delegate to a third person, such as a cleaning person.
7. If there is an activity no one likes, then rotate weekly.

CHART 16: "Like" Scale

Regular home maintenance	Wife	Husband	Child 1	Child 2	Estimated Hours weekly
Dust					
Wash kitchen floor					
Wash bathroom floor					
Clean sinks, bathtubs, toilet bowls					
Clean stove					
Vacuum					
Wash woodwork, windowsills					
Change linens					
Clean refrigerator					
Sweep porch, sidewalk					
Remove clutter					
Wash windows					
Clean mirrors					
Water plants					
Empty garbage					

Time balance—   Wife: Husband: Child 1:   Child 2:

Extra home maintenance	Wife	Husband	Child 1	Child 2	Estimated Hours weekly
Remodeling					
Decorating					
Appliance maintenance					
Lawn (cutting grass, gardening)					
House maintenance repairs					
Sorting children's toys and equipment to organize or dispose of					
Closet cleaning, storeroom cleaning					
Spring cleaning					

Time balance— Wife: Husband: Child 1:   Child 2:

Clothing	Wife	Husband	Child 1	Child 2	Estimated Hours weekly
Deciding children's wardrobe needs					
Shopping for children's clothes, shoes					
Washing					
Drying					
Folding					
Putting away					
Ironing					
Drycleaning					
Alterations					
Changing seasonal clothes					
Straightening and organizing clothes, drawers, closets					

Time balance—   Wife: Husband: Child 1:   Child 2:

CHART 16: "Like"Scale
(continued)

Food	Wife	Husband	Child 1	Child 2	Estimated Hours weekly
Shopping					
Putting groceries away					
Meal planning					
Cooking					
Setting table					
Cleaning up after dinner					
Doing dishes					
Packing children's lunches					
Straightening kitchen					
Sweeping kitchen floor					

Time balance—   Wife: Husband: Child 1:   Child 2:

CHART 16: "Like" Scale
(continued)

Money, paper management	Wife	Husband	Child 1	Child 2	Estimated Hours weekly
Bills					
Insurance (health, life, home, car)					
Taxes					
Stocks					
Bonds					
IRAs					
Installment purchases					
Investments					

Time balance—   Wife: Husband: Child 1:   Child 2:

Family Management	Wife	Husband	Child 1	Child 2	Estimated Hours weekly
Finding and arranging child care					
Car pooling					
Attending school meetings					
Deciding with child on extracurricular activities (arranging schedule for those activities—infant swim, toddler gym, etc.)					
Helping with homework					
Giving children baths					
Arranging doctor and dentist appointments					
Time balance—	Wife:	Husband:	Child 1:	Child 2:	

CHART 16: "Like" Scale
(continued)

Family Management	Wife	Husband	Child 1	Child 2	Estimated Hours weekly
Picking up at day care or school if child sick					
Getting babysitters (nighttime)					
Arranging playtime with other children					
Making arrangements when children have school vacations					
Gift and card buying for special occasions					
Planning business and personal entertainment					
Care of pets					

Time balance—   Wife: Husband: Child 1:   Child 2:

CHART 16: "Like" Scale
(continued)

Car Maintenance	Wife	Husband	Child 1	Child 2	Estimated Hours weekly
Winterizing					
Tires					
General maintenance					
Car repair					
Car license, tags					

Time balance— Wife: Husband: Child 1: Child 2:

Convenience Notebooks

Your mother is watching the kids for the weekend and can't find the toilet paper. Your housekeeper calls you out of an important meeting to tell you that the dishwasher has overflowed. Your wallet is stolen and you must call the credit card companies. We suggest two types of notebooks to help you with these dilemmas:

1. *Home Management Notebook,* which can be used as a reference book by the whole family, your housekeeper, or babysitter. This notebook has all the emergency medical numbers, home maintenance and other important numbers that you frequently use, location of important household items, and instructions on appliance use. This is a working notebook, and items can be added and deleted. We suggest putting it in the kitchen where there is easy access for all.

2. *Personal and Financial Notebook,* containing information on investments, charge accounts, insurance policies, and other important financial matters. This notebook provides you with quick access and an overview of pertinent information. We suggest that this notebook be placed unobtrusively on a bookshelf. If you are planning a trip, you might want to tell a trusted individual where the notebook can be found, or leave it with that person.

Guide: **Home Management Notebook**

Emergency:

Emergency service _____

Ambulance service _____

Fire _____ Police _____

Poison control center _____

Dentist _____

Doctor (children's) _____

Hospital _____

Veterinarian _____

Drug store (prescriptions) _____

    Hours of operation _____

Location of Medical supplies
(Bandaids, first-aid cream) _____

Neighbors _____

_____

Relatives nearby _____

_____

Children's caretaker, schools,
teacher (name of school
phone number, address) _____

_____

_____

Physicians:

Internist _____

Pediatrician _____

Obstetrics and gynecology _____

Opthamologist/Optician _____

Surgeon _____

Cardiologist _____

Therapist _____

Other specialist _____

Children's friends:

Name of friend _____

Name of parents _____

Address and telephone _____

Name of friend _____

Name of parents _____

Address and telephone _____

Name of friend _____

Name of parents _____

Address and telephone _____

Services:

Seamstress, tailor _____

Hairdresser _____

Babysitter _____

Stores:

Bakery _____

Butcher _____

Dry cleaner _____

Grocery store _____

Hardware store _____

Shoe repair _____

Key makers _____

Pizza carry-out _____

Chinese carry-out _____

Delicatessen _____

Other _____

Maintenance:

Air-conditioning repair _____

Appliance dealer and repair (List
individual appliance and
repair shops) _____

_____

_____

_____

_____

Carpenter _____

Carpet cleaner _____

Construction contractor _____

Exterminator _____

Electric company _____

Electrician _____

Furnace repair _____

Gas company _____

Housecleaning _____

Interior decorator _____

Lawn care _____

Mechanic _____

Painter (house) _____

Plumber _____

Roofing repair _____

Telephone company _____

Wallpaper hanger _____

Window cleaner _____

Others _____

_____

_____

_____

_____

_____

City transportation:

Bus _____

Subway _____

Taxi _____

Warranties:

Name of item _____

Where purchased _____

Warranty information _____

_____

Name of item _____

Where purchased _____

Warranty information _____

_____

Name of item _____

Where purchased _____

Warranty information _____

Maintenance agreements with companies:

Item _____

Company _____

When expires _____

Item _____

Company _____

When expires _____

Item _____

Company _____

When expires _____

Location of:

Kitchen appliances _____

_____

_____

Circuits _____

Washing machine/dryer _____

Pots and pans _____

Iron/ironing board _____

Freezer _____

Light bulbs _____

Household cleaners/detergents _____

Paper goods _____

Toiletries (tooth paste, soap) _____

_____

_____

_____

Special instructions on how to operate household appliances _____

_____

_____

_____

_____

_____

_____

_____

Guide: **Personal/Financial Notebook**

Social Security Numbers _____

_____

Automobile:

Car #1 registration No. _____

License plate number _____

Car #2 registration No. _____

License plate number _____

Insurance:

Automobile insurance

Company name and policy number _____

Amount of insurance _____

Address _____

Phone _____

Renewal date _____

Agent _____

Location of policy _____

Health insurance firm

Company name and policy number _____

Amount of insurance _____

Address _____

Phone _____

Renewal Date _____

Agent _____

Location of policy _____

Dental insurance

Company name and policy number _____

Amount of insurance _____

Address _____

Phone _____

Renewal Date _____

Agent _____

Location of Policy _____

Home insurance

Company name and policy number _____

Amount of insurance _____

Address _____

Phone _____

Renewal Date _____

Agent _____

Riders on household items _____

_____

_____

Location of policy _____

Life insurance

Company name and policy number _____

Amount of insurance _____

Address _____

Phone _____

Agent _____

Location of policy _____

Life insurance

Company name and policy number _____

Amount of insurance _____

Address _____

Phone _____

Agent _____

Location of policy _____

Money Management:

Credit card name _____

Account No. _____

Credit line _____

Address _____

Phone _____

Contact person _____

Credit card name _____

Account No. _____

Credit line _____

Address _____

Phone _____

Contact person _____

Credit card name _____

Account No. _____

Credit line _____

Address _____

Phone _____

Contact person _____

Bank Account (savings)

Name of bank _____

Account number _____

Address _____

Phone _____

Contact person _____

Bank Account (checking)

Name of bank _____

Account number _____

Address _____

Phone _____

Contact person _____

Savings bond

Amount _____

Number _____

Maturity date _____

Other bonds

Number, type _____

Maturity date _____

IRA/Keogh accounts

Name of company _____

Account number _____

Interest rate _____

Name of company _____

Account number _____

Interest rate _____

Mutual fund

Name of fund _____

Account number _____

Address _____

Phone _____

Contact person _____

Stocks

Name of stock _____

Name of company _____

Address _____

Phone _____

Name of stockbroker _____

Purchase price _____

Dividends _____

Other Investments

_____

_____

_____

_____

_____

_____

_____

_____

_____

_____

_____

_____

_____

Location of
   Will _____

   Safe deposit box _____

Attorney _____

Address _____

Phone _____

Accountant _____

Address _____

Phone _____

_____

TIPS

The following suggestions come from working parents and will help ease the management of your home. Perhaps you have some tips of your own which you will pass on to us.

- Always carry a small notebook, phone book, and calendar in your pocketbook or briefcase.
- If you have a list of things to remember for the next morning, tape the list to your mirror or purse or exit door.
- Make a "to do" list every day.
- Carry along something you want to do in case you get stuck waiting somewhere—for example, a book or knitting.
- Make a grocery list by category—for example, vegetables, meat, paper products—with room to check off items. Also leave space to mark quantity and the brand-name you prefer. Make photocopies to leave on the refrigerator; check off items needed as you run out and use for grocery shopping list.
- When shopping stock up monthly or bimonthly on staples if budget and storage space allow—then only buy produce or perishables on a weekly basis.
- When cooking, triple or quadruple recipes and freeze.
- A freezer is a must. Prepare food in advance and freeze. Hint—when starting out prepare several of the same recipe at one time. For example, prepare several batches of one recipe the first day. Another day prepare several servings of a second recipe. The third day, cook several dinners of a third recipe. By the end of the week you will have a variety stored that can be used for several weeks. This is more efficient than making five different recipes on Sunday morning for the coming week. It is easier to make five quiches than one chicken, one casserole,

and one quiche all at the same time. As you note you are running out of a particular dish, you can make several more for freezing.

- Order meat in quantities from special meat-packing firms, for example, half a steer cut and packaged.

- For salad, cut up all vegetables you will use in the next few days (carrots, cucumbers, celery, radishes); put each vegetable in a sealed plastic container and take out as much as you need for a salad each night, then add lettuce.

- If you eat simple meals during the week, have a special family meal during the weekend. Use nice dishes and special food, perhaps for a Sunday brunch, lunch or dinner.

- When entertaining, consider having everyone bring a dish.

- Eat on paper plates sometimes.

- Hire a mother's helper, usually a teenager. The helper can do light housework like washing clothes, general straightening, and make lunches for the next day; cook or heat up supper, and watch children while you eat. Mother's helper hours may be from 4 P.M. to 7 P.M. three days a week. It's a big help over the hectic dinner time.

- Use a live-in/work-out housekeeper—if your children are in school and you do not need someone full time at home. An example of this:

7 A.M. to 9 A.M.—housekeeper helps children get up and dress, makes breakfast, straightens house.

4 P.M. to 8 P.M.—housekeeper does laundry, supper, bag lunches, cleans up after dinner, does nighttime babysitting.

Housekeeper works two full days cleaning your home.

Housekeeper does day work in other people's homes the rest of the week.

Advantages for both: you may pay less than full going rate, yet housekeeper actually earns more working in other homes than she would working in your home only.

- Instruction cards. If you hire a non-English-speaking cleaning person it will help to do the following: (1) find someone who knows the language,

(2) have the person write each housecleaning instruction on a 3 x 5 card in both English and the native language: e.g., "wash kitchen floor" in English and Spanish; "clean stove" in English and Spanish. Show the cleaning person only the cards with the particular chores you want done that day. If you are not home, leave the instruction cards on the kitchen table.

- Stock up on gifts to give when invited to someone's house for supper, for example, wine, liquid soap dispensers, fancy pot holders, trivets.

- Buy six unisex gifts to keep on hand for when your child is invited to birthday parties (play dough or finger paints, for instance). Keep wrapping paper in the house, or wrap in newspaper comics or tin foil.

- For birthdays and other special occasions, give a donation to a charity in honor of the person instead of buying a gift.

- Group errands together according to urgency and location.

- Pick out several stores that you like and stay with them. You'll know the layout, the manager, quality of merchandise, and general price range.

- In the kitchen: have a large family kitchen calendar; also a phone book and bulletin board.

- Stay active in one volunteer organization, drop all others. Think carefully about a volunteer activity before committing yourself.

- Get a phone-answering machine. You can avoid interruptions during dinner or when tending to children. Then you can call everyone back when it is convenient for you. Having messages taken when you are out also assures that you do not miss important calls.

- Open a checking account which permits you to pay bills by computer. This cuts time spent writing checks by one-third.

- Have several "in" baskets for bills, correspondence, and magazines. Hint: For more efficient bill paying, look at bill; mark on envelope amount, minimum due, and due date; put latest one on top.

- If you are having problems with time, keep a time record for one week. Examine it to make schedule changes.

- Each child should have a clothes hamper; keep clothes separate while laundering.

Suggested Files

The following are suggested to help organize paperwork and enable you to keep information at your fingertips.

Bills: Put bills paid into a large accordian file under such headings as house utilities, phone, medical bills, donations, store purchases.

Bills pending: File in box for bills that have not been paid.

Charities: For organizations requesting donations—if you don't have money or need to think about whether or not to donate.

Children's school work: Save in a box, later to be put in scrapbook.

Copies of resumes: A job interview might arise—be prepared.

Coupons: You may want to keep this file in your pocketbook or car.

Directions: Put directions to someone's house, or store in a file. You may need them again.

Financial: For information and correspondence that may be sent to you by your banks and investment companies—actual certificates should be put in safe deposit box.

Health: Health certificates, innoculation records, health insurance information.

Household information: Advertisements on carpet cleaning, housepainting, storm windows. You may need them in the future.

Instruction manuals: For example, how to operate new vacuum cleaner, food processor.

Insurance: You may want to keep actual policies in a safe deposit box. This is the file for information and correspondence that companies send. Subjects: house, car, life insurance.

Magazine, newspaper information and articles: Interesting information and news items that you find important.

Miscellaneous: For other important concerns and projects such as redecorating the house; a file for a committee you are serving on.

Occasion cards: Stock up on cards for birthdays, anniversaries, and other special occasions.

Pending—time limited: This includes items that must be acted on—announcement about recreation department activities, classes; announcement about purchasing season tickets for the theater.

Professional: Such as newsletters; notices about conferences, workshops; licensing; job openings.

Receipt file: Save receipts.

Recipes: Recipes from the newspaper, given by friends that you have not had time to place on index cards.

School: Children's school information, directory of classmates, school calendar, PTA bulletin.

Scrapbook: Items you cut out of newspaper or given by friends to be placed in a scrapbook. (You might think you are creating a mess since you probably won't have time to put them in your scrapbook, but at least they will all be in your file should you ever have the time.)

Tax information: Such as information on tax laws and pertinent receipts.

Travel: Advertising and information on vacation resorts, maps, etcetera.

Warranties: All warranties on appliances, watches, and other items.

Parent and Career Issues

In general we have found that working parents feel greatly stressed, particularly at transition points—birth of a new baby, return to work after maternity leave or after years at home, changes in job of either spouse. Of course, such changes are stressful for all parents, and for all people who work. But, because parents with careers have additional role demands, the attendant time constraints, and demands of their work necessitate many more decisions, and additional stresses.

This section contains information and suggestions in brief about some of the major issues faced by working parents. Our purpose is simply to help you to make informed decisions. Topics are arranged alphabetically so you will be able to quickly examine whatever issue is currently of concern to you and our ideas for resolution, and then develop your own solutions.

*   *   *   *

Career in a Holding Pattern

When children are young, both spouses may find it necessary to minimize career changes and career demands in order to avoid extreme stress. For example, you might pick a less challenging job closer to home in order to avoid a long commute. You may reject a challenging, but demanding job that involves overtime or travel because of family commitments. You might put off a training program that would advance you because of its increased time and homework demands. This is what we call career in a "holding pattern."

A holding pattern allows you to meet home responsibilities while still remaining in the job market. You collect a salary, build your resume, and gain experience, but you can walk out the door at 5 P.M. and put work behind you. Although you've put yourself in a holding pattern, you are still ahead of the career game compared to homemakers who have quit work.

Necessity

Many people find that it is difficult to divide their energies between home and work. Every one has a limited energy supply, and it is often difficult to function well in a stressful job and then function equally well at home, with the physical and emotional demands of children. Something must give, and it can be your work or your spouse's work—or both.

Remember that this holding pattern may last only for several years while your children are young. Depending on your particular career and financial needs, this is not long in a lifetime career. Think about it.

Other Considerations

When your children are young you must adjust your job to them. When they are older, they can more easily adjust to your job.

With children, you may not be able to achieve in a career what you would have achieved without them. This is a sacrifice you might make when you decide to have a child, for instance an M.D. who went into research instead of clinical practice because he had children.

As your roles and priorities change because of children, you may feel that you have "abandoned" the work ethic. Although in the past you may have been highly devoted to your career, your primary attention may now be focused toward your children. This can make you feel "guilty" about diverting career ambition.

Also if you choose to put your career in a holding pattern, you may be fearful about whether you will be able to catch up in the job market. You may worry about missed opportunities. But bear in mind that other opportunities will come along, possibly at a time that is more compatible with your needs.

Strategies

We suggest you remain at your current job for at least six months to one year after your baby is born. During this time you are adjusting to your responsibilities and new role as parent. A second adjustment to a new job can add extra stress if you are under pressure for high job performance. If you must change jobs, we suggest the following:

- Choose a sympathetic employer. Someone who will not hassle you about absenteeism when your children are sick. The right employer also will give psychological support and offer opportunities for advancement based on ability.

- Choose a good work environment: a place where colleagues are congenial and the atmosphere is pleasant.

Remember: You must set priorities regarding your level of career commitment according to what is important at each stage of your life.

Child versus Children: Having More Than One

Many couples think about the impact of a second child on their careers and their family responsibilities. With one baby they experienced new time pressures and were forced to reevaluate family and career goals. Working parents must recognize that having another child will involve even more time and career adjustments. Most parents agree that the time-squeeze rises geometrically. For example, look at the relationships involved when there is just one child:

Relationship Chart

Having One Child

Mother } ——— Child 1
Father

Mother ——— Child 1 (Father personal time)

Father ——— Child 1 (Mother personal time)

Mother ——— Father

Having Two Children

Mother
Father $\big\}$ —— Child 1

Mother —— Child 1

Father —— Child 1

Mother
Father $\big\}$ —— Child 2

Mother —— Child 2

Father —— Child 2

Mother —— $\big\{$ Child 1
Child 2 (Father personal time)

Father —— $\big\{$ Child 1
Child 2 (Mother personal time)

Mother
Father $\big\}$ —— $\big\{$ Child 1
Child 2

Mother —— Father

It is, as the chart illustrates, important for each parent to spend time alone with each child, and important for there to be "family" time when the whole family is together. With one child, each parent is able to have some personal time while the other parent is with the child. With two children this personal time is diminished, since each parent may be occupied with the needs of a child. Moreover, this chart does not show the increased home- and family-management responsibilities.

In addition to the effect on relationships, having additional children means:

- Changes in lifestyle. You will have less mobility (it's easier to take one child to a restaurant, museum, or on a trip). The differing needs and interests of each child must also be balanced within a limited timeframe. There is less time for personal hobbies and activities.

- Day Care. Even if children are close in age, two different kinds of day-care arrangements may be needed, depending on the needs of each child.

- Changes in parenting. You have learned how to deal with a particular first child. If the second child is similar, then the same techniques will work; if the child is different (and this is usually so), then it is necessary to learn new methods and devise new strategies. This takes lots of time and energy.

  No matter how much you have prepared your first child for the arrival of a baby, expect some negative reactions. You will have to work hard with your first child.

  Spouse support and a harmonious relationship are most essential in the first six months after a second child arrives. You will have to concentrate on your marital relationship.

- Effects on careers. Due to the increased time and energy pressures, be prepared to keep your career in a holding pattern. If possible, plan to have a second child around a time of less career pressure.

We have seen a high dropout rate of women from the work force when they have their second child (assuming both children are preschool age). The rise in the home workload, the readjustment in family relationships, and the time-pressures all help create mental and emotional stress. Something has to give. While calling in extra help—such as a live-in housekeeper or cleaning person—can be a solution, women at the lower end of the pay scale often find their salaries eaten up. In addition, contending with the pressures of home and work may not appear to be worth the effort for at least a few years. At this point, you could consider the possibility of part-time work. However, many women previously opted for part-time work after the birth of a first child, so there are fewer alternatives when the second is born.

Our advice is not to make hasty decisions about quitting work. Think over your options carefully. Review your budget, flexibility of your job, possibilities for nonpaid help (for instance, trading babysitting with other parents). Anticipate and renegotiate changes in your home-management techniques and your marital relationship.

Speaking from experience with two children, we have to add a positive note. It is a joy to see two children grow: to care for and play with each other (a three-year-old will sometimes entertain an infant long after you have tired); to watch them test their relationships with each other, thus broadening their horizons beyond their parents; to try new techniques with a second child that never occurred to you with the first (and hopefully making fewer mistakes); and to increase, geometrically, the amount of love, caring, giving, and plain fun, in your household.

Competition for Time

No matter how organized you are, you and your spouse will probably experience competition for personal time and space. As we suggested earlier, the only way to guarantee some private time is to schedule it. The question may arise—What is the definition of private time? This is an issue which you and your spouse need to discuss. Does private time include certain personal necessity time such as time to exercise, personal clothes shopping or does private time mean time to indulge in a massage, or lunch with friends? Private time should include only time spent on oneself, rather than errand running or job related activities. You and your spouse will find yourselves trying to schedule your own personal time. This constant juggling and rejuggling of a very limited commodity often becomes an issue between spouses.

First, do the obvious. Look to cut corners when allocating time for yourself. Can you shop during your lunch hour for a new coat? Can you exercise in a nearby gym during your lunch hour or during your children's nap time on a weekend? Look to find ways to make it easier on your spouse when you take time off.

Also recognize that time allocations may be different from week to week depending on your work schedules and the schedules of your children. Be flexible. It is not necessary that there be a quid pro quo every week.

But if you find that you are fighting about time, make a time chart. Post it on the refrigerator for two or three weeks. Keep track of how much personal time has been allowed each spouse. Using something "objective" is often the best way to avoid disagreements.

Look at our sample chart (Chart 17A, page 127). Each spouse should have a separate chart. Each chart should note the date, the specific time of the day, the amount of time that was spent and how it was spent.

CHART 17A: Competition Time Chart
(Sample)

Husband

DAY/DATE	TIME	AMOUNT	FOR WHAT
Mon. 1/28	6-7 p.m.	1 hour	jog
Thurs. 1/31	7-9 p.m.	2 hours	clothes shopping

CHART 17B: Competition Time Chart
(Wife)

DAY/DATE	TIME	AMOUNT	FOR WHAT

CHART 17C: Competition Time Chart
(Husband)

DAY/DATE	TIME	AMOUNT	FOR WHAT

Couple Communications

We have emphasized that the most important point in the family-career balance is communication between partners. The word "communication" is overused. Children and parents don't "communicate." Neither do employer and employee. What is communication? Basically, it is a system for sending and receiving messages. The sender should give a clear message that the receiver can understand and interpret in the manner that the sender intended.

When we refer to couple communication, we are referring to clear messages sent and received on an adult level—adult to adult. Both of you are making free and equal exchanges. There are no hidden agendas; no harbored ill feelings; no attempts to "get back" at the other one. Each of you is able to express feelings openly and honestly about an issue. Each of you knows that your opinion will be respected. You are prepared to compromise. There is no such thing as "winning," "losing" or "putting something over on someone."

Dual-career couples usually have trouble finding the right moment to communicate. Mornings are hectic and the conversation focuses on getting everyone out of the house. In the evening there is the rush for dinner and the attendant chores of cleaning up and meeting the children's needs. Then there is often collapse, and escape to the television.

We suggest that you set aside 15 minutes every night for couple-communication time. This should be viewed as a preventive mechanism in that it does not allow resentment or anger between you and your spouse to build up over a period of time. It can also prevent bursts of anger at inopportune times. You can contain momentary anger as your spouse is departing for work, because you know you will have communication time that evening. Most important, with a specific time for communication, it is less likely that someone will go to bed angry.

Decisions: How to Make Them

Let's say you are offered a new job. But there are some negative aspects, and you're not sure whether to accept. Use a decision chart. Of course, we don't expect you to make a decision based only on the chart, but it is a good starting point for considering the issues that concern you. The chart is divided into "pros" and "cons" and "objective" and "subjective" issues. The objectives are usually concrete while the subjectives represent feelings. Although we try to make a decision objectively, we cannot deny our emotional or gut reactions to an issue. In this chart, the objective issues are given more weight.

On the sample (Chart 18A, page 131), "prestige" and "challenge" are listed as subjective since they are not specifically concrete in this job offer. Under cons, the fear of criticism or not being able to do the job is recognized. How would you rate that fear? In the sample chart, the pros "won," but it was close. Attached is a chart for your own decision making. It will help put the issue in perspective.

Does Money Equal Tired?

The saying that "money is power" is firmly entrenched in our beliefs as a society. Couples usually feel that the partner who makes the most money has the most important job. Many couples may also assume that the partner who makes the most money holds the power in terms of decision making, time allocations, and the financial aspects of the marriage. One belief is that the partner who makes the most money also works the hardest, is under the most pressure, and has the right to be more tired. This exempts him or her from home management or child rearing responsibilities. In some instances, this can be true. One can have exceptionally long hours, be under enormous pressures, and have little time flexibility. In this case, the home manager has more responsibility to keep the home fires burning.

Examine your situation. Is there an equal division of labor based on differing job and home requirements? Or is there failure to share the load? Although you may not earn as much as your spouse, you may be just as tired, work just as hard, and have just as many job pressures. Tiredness and pressures are subjective. Who do you think is most tired? A nurse, a grocery check-out clerk, a dentist, or a top executive? Don't get into a battle with your spouse over this. Discuss the fact that you are both working for the family and making a contribution to the family income. Both of you deserve respect for your work and efforts made. The children belong to both of you. You both want to participate in their upbringing. You might use the "Change Chart" or "Like Scale." Also don't hesitate to hire help if you can.

(continued on page 133)

CHART 18A: **Decision Chart (Sample)**

New Job

PROS

Objective

More money—10

Meet new people—7

Opportunty to do something different—8

Opportunity to move up the career ladder—9

New boss seems nice; good to work with—8

42

Subjective

Prestige—5

Challenging—5

10

Total Score Pros: 52

CONS

Objective

Stressful aspects—6

Overtime—7

25 percent travel—8

Seasonal deadlines—6

Can be easily fired—10

37

Subjective

Fear of not being able to meet challenge—5

Fear of criticism—4

9

Total Score Cons: 46

1. Weight each *objective* on a scale of 6 to 10 with 10 being most important to you and 6 least important.
2. Weight each *subjective* on a scale of 1 to 5 with 5 being the most important to you and 1 least important.
3. Add up all the pros (objective plus subjective).
4. Add up all the cons (objective plus subjective).
5. Compare the pros and cons—the highest score wins.

CHART 18B: Decision Chart

PROS

Objective   *Subjective*

CONS

Objective   *Subjective*

(continued from page 130)

Your physical and mental health are important. Decide together what extras you are willing to forgo if you hire help. You will have to make trade-offs, but make them together.

Family Management and Communication: Tips

- On Saturday night lay out a simple Sunday breakfast for your preschoolers. A four-year-old can pour milk from a small container into a cereal bowl already filled with cereal. A baggie with cut and peeled fruit or bread and butter completes the breakfast. This allows you an extra snooze on Sunday mornings.

- Want a peaceful dinner with your spouse? Give your children a special (not too messy) dessert in their room or playroom. Or give a new toy or book as a special "earned" treat. Enjoy your meal (quietly).

- Trade off Sundays once a month with someone who has children similar to the ages of yours.

- Combine errands with spouse communication—go out for coffee on Friday night, then do food shopping with your spouse.

- Meet your spouse for a formal lunch during the workday.

- Get up an hour earlier than your children and spouse. Do something that *you* enjoy that you can't do with "company."

- While giving your young child a bath, ask about the day with the sitter or at school. Children are relaxed—and receptive—in the bathtub!

- One night a week sit down with your spouse in a different place in your house, and discuss events at work, mutual interests, and social plans. Talk of problems with children or home is not allowed.

Getting Along with Mothers who Work at Home

Some of the feelings that may contribute to feelings of stress and guilt can be attributed to the very complicated relationship we working parents (primarily women) have with women who stay at home full-time. More than differing schedules and possibly income, attitudes and opinions between the two groups often seem to be at two ends of the spectrum. There are good reasons for these strong feelings. More importantly, there are even better reasons for working to close this gap.

In the late 1960's and early 1970's, women of all ages experienced great pressures to maintain or embark on careers. Stay-at-home women felt pressures to return to work, and women working out of their homes naively assumed an easy continuance of their employment along with major changes in lifestyle, such as marriage and children. In recent years we have seen a sweep of the pendulum, with many employed women feeling pressured to quit the job market and return home. In each case, the feelings of antipathy, jealousy and resentment have remained. Some stay-at-home mothers claim that they bear the brunt of carpools, school and community volunteer work because they sacrifice their careers and additional income and stay home with their children. Employed mothers are on the defensive and cite studies demonstrating that their children do not suffer from substitute care, and that they devote more "quality" time to their children than do stay-at-home mothers.

As more and more parents find part-time work a good alternative, some of these differences will blur. But right now we can ease the tension by changing our own behavior. Here are a few suggestions. We'd welcome hearing your ideas!

- Try trading off with at-home moms. Offer to take their child on an outing (or babysit) on a weekend or your day off, if they will reciprocate by carpooling for an agreed-upon period of time, for you.

- Arrange some outings together, with the children, on weekends or days off. This will get the children—and you—together.

- Although we have advised you to limit your volunteer work, select an activity to work on that can be done on a weekend or evening, that is time-limited, yet useful to your child's school or organization. You will gain points with your child, as well as taking some of the burden off the more available moms.

- Try to exchange some erranding. Offer to pick up cleaning if the cleaner is on your way home from work. Your stay-at-home neighbor could let your painter in for you at 4:30 and wait until you returned home at 5:00.

Guilt and Stress

- I feel guilty when I spend an hour having a facial. I should be with my kids.

- I am tired when I get up at 6 A.M. for a sunrise swim—but there's no other time to exercise.
- I feel guilty when the teacher calls to tell me that my child is misbehaving in school.
- I feel badly when I can't go on field trips with my child.
- I waited to take my child to the doctor when she was feeling ill; I thought it was a 24-hour virus and it was strep throat instead. I feel guilty.
- I get frustrated when I shop for clothes and cannot find anything that looks good on me.
- I get upset when I shop for clothes and everything is too expensive.
- I get angry when I shop for summer clothes and the stores are already showing winter clothes.
- I hate waiting in line at the supermarket.
- I hate coming home to dirty dishes and unmade beds after a day at work.
- I hate staying up late at night to do the bills.
- I feel guilty going away for the weekend with my spouse and leaving the kids.
- No one liked what I cooked for supper tonight.
- I wish I could eat my supper in peace.
- I feel guilty when I arrive two hours late for work—school started late because of snow.
- I rush out of work to bring my child the lunch he left in the car.

The main source of stress and guilt is role conflict caused by demands we make on ourselves and the demands others make on us. Career, family, and personal roles become confused. Your best response to these feelings is to recognize and sort out these demands as early as possible, and make conscious compromises. Remember that guilt feelings are forever present, whether you are working or not, and these feelings always seem to catch us at a vulnerable moment.

The ability to control stress and guilt is often intertwined with your motivation to work and your commitment to a career. It is therefore important that you carefully assess your career and personal goals. It is easy to drop out of the work force during peak feelings of stress or guilt if you do not have firm career goals.

Definitions

Guilt feelings, which are often tied to unrealistic expectations, are dynamic. They involve feelings of self-blame and are major stress-producers.

Stress can be understood as an overload of demands causing tension, and sometimes "burn-out" in an individual. Guilt and stress often go hand-in-hand, one causing the other. Stress and guilt are also *opportunity signals* to make changes in your lifestyle.

Sources of guilt and stress:

- Major role conflicts between career, family, and personal needs.

- Too many changes at one time: addition of new family member; move to new home; career or job change.

- Demands of other people on us: for example, family members with differing expectations of our roles; or coworkers with certain expectations of our responsibilities.

- Our own expectation of ourselves: we are indeed our own worst enemies, sometimes!

Recognizing some symptoms of guilt and stress: fatigue and feelings of exhaustion; overwhelming feeling of too much to do and not knowing where to begin; difficulty in coping with everyday problems at work and home; inability to think clearly—head full of "cob webs."

Handling guilt and stress: In dealing with role conflict—which causes guilt and stress—list your major roles, your priorities, and the time you currently spend in each "role." Look for discrepancies between priorities and time spent, and try to make changes in your time allotments. Sometimes "quantity time" is also important! Other things to do:

- Learn to make the transition from one role—to "turn off"—and "turn on" to another. It's important to turn quickly at the beginning of the day from parent to worker and at the end of the day from worker to parent. (See Chart 19 on page 137 to pinpoint stressful times in your day.)

- Examine the situation. Is family and home management overwhelming? Are there too many work tensions? Initiate solutions.

(continued on page 138)

CHART 19: Transition Points of Stress During the Workday

The following are transition points during the workday which can be stressful. This chart will help you to pinpoint your most stressful time.

	Very stressful	Moderately stressful	Somewhat stressful	Not stressful at all
Morning time (getting up, getting kids dressed, getting out of house)				
Taking kids to school or day care				
Commuting time to work				
Arrival at place of work—(Do you have time for coffee to unwind from your commute? Do your co-workers or boss present you with immediate deadlines? Are there work crises that you must attend to?)				
Lunch time (Do you eat a leisurely lunch? Are you running errands? Are you doing catch-up work?)				
Leaving office (Do you feel things are half done when you leave? Are you rushing out to pick up child?)				
Commute time (back home)				
Picking up kids from school or day care				
Coming home (Are you frantically trying to fix dinner with kids vying for attention?)				
After dinner clean-up				
Preparing for bedtime—baths, reading stories to kids.				

(continued from page 136)

- Don't be defensive about your decision to work. Treat your relationships with your housekeeper, nursery school teacher, co-workers, and boss as "normal." Don't view *yourself* as guilty or conflicted and you won't be viewed that way.

- Don't use your job as a scapegoat. "If I were at home: Susan would not have broken her arm; Johnny would do his homework and improve his grades." Remember: parents who don't work feel guilty, too. It goes with the territory.

- Take time-out. Devote one full day to yourself. Go to the sauna, have a massage, go to the library. Think of this as mental health dollars spent for your whole family.

- Ask yourself if the principles and rules prescribed by parents, friends, teachers, and society are sound and sensible and you believe them. Or, are they unwarranted and outdated? Remember, if you followed every one else's advice, you'd be going in 20 different directions!

- Ask yourself if there are other ways to meet some of these demands. For instance, if you cannot volunteer during the day in your child's school, suggest certain volunteer activities that you can accomplish at night, such as telephone calls. Try to choose something that is somehow visible to your child.

- Evaluate your own expectations.

Many women, and men, are brought up with the conditioned response that "good mothers" take care of "home and children." Thus, these women who go to work take on two full-time jobs because relinquishing any responsibilities at home produces great guilt. The result is the "super-woman" complex, along with more guilt and stress. There aren't any perfect children, just as there aren't any perfect mothers and fathers. Children with at-home mothers or fathers are not very different from children of working mothers. Therefore, don't fall into the trap of overindulging or over-protecting your children to "compensate" for your time away from them.

Help! When to See an Expert

The words therapy, counseling, support groups, social worker, psychiatrist, and psychologist sometimes evoke stereotyped images. What's wrong with you? Why can't you handle your own problems? More guilt! We urge you to put aside these feelings. Don't look at the need to seek professional help as an admission of failure, but as an opportunity to grow and change. After all, you are carrying a heavy load and have lots of stress and pressures. In parenting and working you're pioneering new territory for which there are few roadmaps.

The main point is not to wait until you are "in crisis." We believe in preventive maintenance. If you ignore a problem hoping things will get better on their own, the situation will often get worse and take much longer to repair.

We first believe in self-help. A women's, or men's or couple's support group focusing on the working parent can give you an outlet to voice your concerns. You can see how others are doing things, hear about the problems they have, and together make attempts to resolve issues. In addition a support group can become your support network to call on in time of special need.

But you may need more than a support group can offer. How do you know when you need professional help? Here are some signs to consider, if they last longer than a month:

- Individual problem
  - Feeling depressed
  - Days missed from work because of psychosomatic complaints or feelings of just not wanting to get up
  - Frequent mood swings: highly excited, then blue; emotions easily aroused—flying off the handle, crying
  - Relationship problems which have not been resolved (with spouse, friend, lover, boss, parents)
  - Feelings that you want to harm yourself, your child or other people
  - Sudden change in your life, for example, death in the family, divorce, loss of job, birth of child, or move to a new home
- Problem with child
  - Developmental stage according to chronological age appears slow: i.e., child is not talking or walking when you think he should (contact a physician)
  - Difficulty in getting along well with other children or teacher
  - Difficulty in sitting or paying attention

— A loner
— Emotional flare-ups with extreme tantrums occurring often
— Phobic reactions such as not wanting to go to school or day care

It should be noted that at certain stages in a child's development there are typical behavioral and emotional difficulties. So ask yourself these questions when considering professional help for a child:
— Is this problem typical at the age and stage of my child's development?
— How long has this problem been going on?
— Is it getting better or worse?
— Has this problem developed as a result of family stress?
— How have I tried to resolve the problem? Is there anything else I could do? Am I and my spouse in agreement on how to resolve the problem?

- Marital problems
  — You feel that you and your spouse can't "communicate"
  — You can't honestly express your feelings with your spouse.
  — You feel that decision-making is not shared in your marriage.
  — You feel that both of you are not giving and getting your fair share in the marriage.
  — You feel competitive toward your spouse; jealous of his or her achievements.
  — You harbor feelings of anger or resentment toward your spouse.
  — Your feelings toward your spouse have changed.
  — One of you is having an affair.
  — You don't have time to be together.
  — Your spouse is not interested in the things you do or your career.

If you want to help your marriage, it's always best to go to a professional as a couple. However, if one partner refuses, go alone. You may be able to gather insight into the situation, and make some changes which can help the whole family. Your spouse may decide to go later when she or he doesn't feel so threatened by the situation.

In examining problems, recognize their interactions. For example, you may feel depressed. This feeling of depression could be in response to harbored feelings of uncommunicated anger and resentment toward your spouse. Or the noncommunication between you and your spouse could reflect itself in the behavior of your child. Try to examine the situation carefully to pinpoint your problem. Remember, too, that professional help need not be long-term. Often a few sessions can be of enormous help.

Long-Distance Commuting

You just got a terrific job offer in another city. Your spouse's current work situation is very satisfactory and offers many opportunities for advancement. What do you do? Think over the following issues:

1. Does the job offer look like a "permanent" position? How stable is the company? Has the company had a great deal of staff turnover? Is it in the red? Are you looking at the job from a realistic point of view? How well do you think you will get along with your new colleagues and boss? A commuting arrangement gives you time to "feel out" the job.

2. If you do commute, how long do you expect this arrangement to last? Put a time limit on it.

3. What kind of extra stress will this arrangement have on the children? On your spouse?

4. How often will you be able to return to the family? How often will they be able to visit you?

5. Consider your relationship with others during the commuting period. What kind of behavior do you expect from each other during this time?

6. How much will the commuting arrangement cost you? Consider costs of housing and transportation.

There needs to be more research done on the effects of long-distance commuting on marriage and the children. But it is clear that many factors must enter into the decision to commute in order to make it a successful option.

Marriage Contract for Dual-Career Couples

Writing a marriage contract has become popular today. The process of writing a contract can help you to realistically examine your expectations of your marriage, each other, and of yourself.

There are particular issues which need to be addressed by you as a dual-career couple. Unless confronted and negotiated these issues are liable to cause extra strain on your marriage, misunderstanding between you and your spouse, and unwarranted aggravation, anger, and hurt.

The process of developing a contract is as important as the contract itself since it involves negotiation and compromise. This process may also prevent future problems. If you and your spouse disagree about an issue, it is easy to refer to the contract and renegotiate if necessary. The contract should also help assure a sense of equality in your decision-making process.

The following subjects should be incorporated into a dual-career couple's contract:

- Set compatible career goals as a dual-career couple. Does one partner aim for Capitol Hill while the other aims for Wall Street?
- Determine whose career comes first. Whose career is considered more important? This can be a painful process, but it must be addressed. Numerous day-to-day decisions are most easily made if this key decision has already been made: who will work overtime, take extra training programs and the like.
- Negotiate family management. Who stays home when children are sick? Who takes them to doctor and dentist appointment? Who drives car pools? Who goes to parent-teacher conferences and PTA meetings?
- Determine who has responsibility for ongoing child-care issues. Who hires the child care provider? Who finds the nursery school or day care center? Who meets periodically with the caretaker? Who pays and negotiates changes in pay, benefits, and responsibilities of the caretaker?
- Determine how finances will be handled. Will there be joint or separate accounts? Whose money will be used for which expenses?
- Arrange for household management: Who does what chores? When? According to whose standards?
- Set compatible personal goals (these may be different from career goals), including exercise, hobbies, free time, and friends. Ask yourself: Are career, personal and family goals compatible? Practical? Achievable?
- Schedule set days and times for personal time for each partner.
- Agree on how family time will be spent. What kinds of things do you want to do as a family? When? How much time will be spent?

- Consider volunteer organizations: How much time will be spent with them?
- Review the business and social obligations of each partner. How often are you expected to entertain business acquaintances, attend functions, etcetera?

Set a time, we suggest six months, to reevaluate the contract.

Nursing and Working

It is possible to nurse your baby and work. We encourage all mothers to nurse their babies if possible since breast milk is superior to formula. However, a word of caution: breast-feeding can be exhausting. After all, the baby is taking fluid from your body, and in order to build up your milk supply, you will need to: (1) pump milk often; (2) get plenty of rest; and (3) drink lots of fluids. Stress that you feel on the job or at home can contribute to a decreased milk supply. Therefore, we suggest that if you plan to nurse, if possible, take the optimal six months off or ease your way back to work on a part-time basis during the first six months. By six months your baby may be on solids and the demand for milk will decrease.

Some suggestions for nursing and working:

- Use a breast pump. (We suggest the Loyd-B-Pump by Lopuco. Check with a local hospital or the local La Leche League about where you can obtain one.)
- When pumping, put milk in plastic or glass baby bottle or Playtex nurser bags; place in refrigerator. Fresh milk must be used within 24 hours or frozen as soon as possible after pumping.
- Freeze milk in plastic or glass baby bottle or Playtex nurser bottle bags. Frozen milk should be used within six months.
- If possible nurse your baby during your lunch break.
- In order to have enough milk you must pump the same number of times during the day that the baby drinks; e.g., if your baby feeds three times when you are gone, then you should pump at approximately the times of those feedings. This is necessary to keep up your milk supply. Do not be discouraged if you are unable to pump as much milk as the baby drinks. Pump whatever you can. Just be sure to pump or your milk supply will dry up.

- If you find nursing exhausting, or it is too difficult to pump, consider nursing only morning and evening and substituting formula when you are at work. Get your doctor's recommendation on the type of formula to use. This way you can still give your baby the benefit of nursing and feel more free during the day. Your milk supply will readjust automatically within a few days.

- Breast-feeding can leave you exhausted. Also your hormones usually do not return to their normal pre-pregnancy state during nursing, so you may find yourself oversensitive to issues that normally would not bother you. This in combination with fatigue can be overwhelming.

- It is important that you drink at least eight, eight-ounce glasses of liquid a day.

- In order to pump milk, you should seek privacy and a comfortable place. Some workplaces may not have adequate facilities to pump (e.g., dirty restrooms).

- Pumping milk can take 10 to 20 minutes at a time. In an eight-hour day you may miss two to three feedings. Some women do not have the time available for pumping during their workday.

- Bottles: babies who drink from the breast and bottle may prefer the bottle because it is easier to suck. They may reject the breast and begin to wean themselves. Hint: put the bottle in baby's mouth for the first two minutes, then switch quickly to breast.

- On the other hand, your baby may prefer the breast to the bottle. If you know you will be returning to work within six weeks of the birth, you should give the baby at least one bottle a day right away. Otherwise, allow two weeks for adjustment to the bottle. Hint: sometimes the baby takes a bottle more easily from someone other than the mother. If the baby won't take the bottle, give the breast first for two minutes then switch quickly to bottle.

We recommend nursing full- or part-time for as long as you feel comfortable. You may have some problems initially adjusting to working and nursing, but don't give up quickly. Seek support and additional advice from other mothers and various parent-child associations in your area.

Parents: To Be or Not to Be

You may not be a parent but may be in the process of weighing the pros and cons of parenthood. Perhaps you bought this book for information on how to manage career and parenthood if you decide to have a baby. You may hear the biological clock ticking and feel pressure; or maybe your partner wants a baby and you don't; or perhaps you need some support for a decision you have already made.

The decision to become a parent is probably the most irreversible decision you will make in your life. Although you can attempt to be objective about it, the decision is laden with emotion. If you are having trouble making a decision, workshops and consulting a professional can aid you. These can help you to view the situation objectively and help you to explore some of your inner feelings about becoming a parent.

Here we offer you some exercises to help in reaching a decision.

1. *Pros and cons of parenthood*
   You and your partner should separately list your reasons for having and not having children. You may notice that the reasons for not having children, such as financial and career, are tangible reasons whereas the reasons for having children are intangible such as love, the desires for giving, and immortality. Discuss the lists together.

2. *Family of origin*
   - Each partner should separately examine the model of his and her own parents and relatives.
   - List things about your parents that you would want to emulate as a parent yourself.
   - List things about your parents that you want to reject.

   Did one partner have extremely negative family experiences while growing up? Did one partner have positive experiences? Think of family circumstances which may have shaped your parents' actions and your own feelings towards them as a child, e.g., divorce, financial constraints, death. These could be key to decision-making.

3. *Child-rearing philosophy*
   Both partners should list their ideas on child-rearing.
   - Does one of you believe that children should be "seen and not heard" while the other expects activity and noise?

- Do you think the family should be run autocratically or that a child can "participate" in some family decision-making?
- Who should discipline? What type of discipline?
- What part do you feel religion should play in your child's life?
- What kind of education do you want for your child?
- How would you feel if your child is not "bright"?
- How much time should you spend with a child? How much family time?
- How well do you relate to children?

4. *Goals as an individual/goals as a couple*

Both partners should separately write down their individual goals and compare them.

- Together, write down your goals as a couple.
- Both partners should list separately the changes and adjustments they would have to make as individuals and together as a couple (see the issues under "Marriage contract") with the addition of a baby.
- Can your goals as an individual and as a couple be fulfilled if you have a child?
- Are you willing to make compromises?

The demands of a child and the demands of a career are basically incompatible. If you think that you can have a child and proceed with your life as before, you will be in for a rude awakening. Two A.M. feedings are not conducive to alertness at an 8 A.M. business meeting. Are both of you willing to put your family ahead of your career? How flexible are you as an individual, as a couple? Are you adaptable to changes? Can you tolerate an unpredictable lifestyle?

5. *Scenarios*

Each partner should write the following scenarios:

- What will my life be like if I do not have children?
- What will it be like if I do?
- Will I have any regrets if I do have children?
- What will they be?
- Will I have any regrets if I don't have children?
- What will those regrets be?

This last exercise is probably the most helpful one. Try to be as honest and open with yourself as you can.

Part-time versus Full-time Work

Chart 20 which follows shows the advantages and disadvantages of part-time and full-time employment. If you are considering part-time work, it is important for you to know precisely why you want to work part-time.

Ask yourself these questions: Do I want to spend more time with my children? Do I need more time for home management? Is combining full-time work and family obligations too much stress for me?

Examine the sources of stress. Are they self-imposed or coming from outside sources? Can they be alleviated in ways other than switching to part-time work?

Can your spouse modify her or his work schedule to accommodate your working full-time and family obligations?

If you are going to work part-time in order to be with your children more—make sure that you allow for this when you create more free time. Your family should understand this. Too often, the person who works part-time takes on increased home and family management responsibilities and neglects the quality time that was initially sought. One way to avoid this is to carefully schedule activities with your children. The "scheduled" time does not have to be for formal activities, such as classes. You can schedule this time for informal at-home activities. The key is to set aside time to be shared with your children.

Work Structure

If it is possible to structure your own part-time hours, we suggest that you work a reduced number of whole days rather than part days for the following reasons:

- It is easier to find day care for whole days.
- It is easier to get more work done in large blocks of time.
- A work emergency won't come up just as you are leaving the office at 2 P.M.
- You save money on transportation.
- You save time due to decreased commuting.

(continued on page 149)

CHART 20: Part-time versus Full-time Work

	Part-time	Full-time
Advantages	Flexibility Less separation from children Keep up with your field Uninterrupted work—looks better on resume than no work at all	Easier to find full-time jobs and and child care More benefits Looks better on your resume Better salary Career advancement
Disadvantages	Job pressure—often work is not reduced proportionately to the number of hours in work week Pay is lower Benefits not as good Cannot advance as quickly More difficult to find part-time work More difficult to find part-time child care Family demands more household management responsibilities from you since you are working part-time.	May spend more money because you don't have time to clean house, search out competitive prices, etcetera. Less time with children Must plan time very carefully May feel more stress in conflicting role demands May not have much time to socialize with friends or pursue outside activities

(continued from page 147)

Another word of caution: because of limited funds, employers often hire a part-time employee for a job that requires full-time effort. Make sure that your employer is not expecting the same amount of work as from a full-time employee. Examine the job description critically, and ask appropriate questions at the time of the interview.

Pediatricians: How to Choose

You have returned to work and have a hectic schedule. Two A.M. feedings, breast-feeding itself, and job demands have left you exhausted. You take your infant to the pediatrician for a well-baby checkup. During the visit the pediatrician tells you that your baby has not gained much weight since the last checkup. The following could then take place:

1. Your pediatrician tells you that the small weight gain could indicate serious problems, or it could be that your baby has reached a brief plateau. The pediatrician questions you closely on your baby's nursing habits and how much the baby drinks. The doctor implies that maybe your caretaker may be doing something wrong and it's your responsibility to see that the baby has proper care. The doctor also suggests that you stop breast-feeding since your baby is probably not getting enough milk. The doctor is not supportive of your working. The visit makes you feel extremely guilty and suspicious of your caretaker. You think about quitting work.

2. Your pediatrician tells you that the small weight gain could indicate serious problems or it could be that your baby has reached a brief plateau. The pediatrician discusses your baby's schedule and feeding habits and gives you suggestions, such as demand feedings (or waking your baby up to eat if the baby is a sleeper). The pediatrician encourages breast-feeding, but suggests that you might supplement with formula or solid foods, depending on the baby's age. The doctor is supportive of your working, and tells you to come back in two weeks for a weight check. You will discuss the situation with your caretaker and keep an eye on the situation. You may decide to take a few days off to rest in order to replenish your milk supply.

These scenarios point to the importance of selecting a pediatrician who is not only competent, but who will also be supportive of working parents and supportive of breast-feeding. You also want a pediatrician who can make some accommodations to working parents regarding office hours and phone availability. We suggest that you make a prenatal visit to several pediatricians (expect to pay for the physician's consultation time) prior to selecting one. Obtain names of pediatricians from your friends and the local American Medical Association.

To make a judgment on the doctor's competency and compatibility with your philosophy as a working parent, consider asking the following:

1. When graduated?
2. Training and years of experience?
3. Subspecialty?
4. Is it a group or solo practice?
   If solo, who will cover for the doctor? Will it be the same person all the time? Who is it? What is that person's background and training? If a group practice, how does the group operate? Who is in the practice? What are their backgrounds and training? Is someone available at all times? Can you see a particular person in the practice? Do you have to take whoever is available?
5. What hospital is the doctor associated with?
6. Are there Saturday office hours for well or sick babies? Are there nighttime hours?
7. What is the doctor's philosophy about breast-feeding? What has his or her experience been with breast-feeding mothers?
8. How does the doctor feel about working mothers? What has the doctor's experience been with working and nonworking mothers?
9. Is there a physician's assistant or nurse clinician available to speak to about general problems?
10. Does the doctor have a call-in hour when you can discuss general concerns about your baby?
11. What are the fees?

Quitting a Job—or Not

If I quit, I'll never be able to regain my job.
If I don't quit, my marriage will go down the tubes.

If I quit, I'll never attain the same career status.

If I don't quit, my kids will know their sitter better than they know me.

If I quit, it will be difficult to attain the same salary level again.

If I don't quit, I'll lose the respect of my boss and co-workers due to my deteriorating performance on the job.

If I quit, I'll go crazy at home.

If I don't quit, I'll have accrued loads of social security and retirement benefits.

If I quit, I will damage my self-image.

If I quit, I will damage the image my spouse has of me.

If I quit, Suzie will get better grades and Johnny won't misbehave in school.

If I don't quit, I'll die of exhaustion, and then there won't be any choice to make at all.

The time comes when the temptation to quit the working-parent merry-go-round rears its head. What to do? Assess your feelings honestly. How much do you need the money? Can other alterations be made in the family budget? Maybe there are budget changes that you can make that have not been previously considered. Are you working for your self-image? Can you do something else that will take less time away from home? Are you quitting to be with your kids more, for more personal time, or for more time with your spouse? Would you *really* spend more time with your family? Are you having marital problems due to your working—or are there other unresolved issues in your marriage? Are your job skills and job status very dependent on the current market? With either part-time or volunteer work, could you keep up with your field and re-enter at a future date? Are you willing to adjust your career goals to meet the demands of your family? What specifically do you want to do with your time? How will others' expectations of you change?

Of course, no one can tell you what to do. But a few suggestions:

• Take some time off if possible, and sample a different lifestyle. If you can't take time off, question friends who are doing things differently about their daily activities, and their reasons for choosing a different style.

- Lay out plans: How would you spend your time? Would you pursue a different, less challenging or less time-consuming career? Would you immerse yourself in your children's activities, volunteer activities, school?

    It might be helpful to draw a sample calendar of activities for a week. Put it away for awhile, then look at it again after talking with friends, and mentally "try it on for size."

- Remember that you have a lot of working years to regain a certain status or commitment to your work. Your children are young for only a relatively short period. Try to keep a long-term perspective.

- It is sometimes a good idea to move on to something new. You may have thought of changing careers before you had children, and this may be the "push" you need to make a move. (Beware of jumping from the frying pan into the fire, however. *Don't* expect to go into something new and hope to give it all your energy.) Maybe a career change is the real reason you are quitting your present job?

- If you do quit, keep your hand in something related to your former work. Attend conferences, keep up contacts with colleagues, read the journals.

- If you feel the slightest hesitation about quitting—don't. You may only be feeling momentarily overwhelmed. You might have a particularly difficult assignment at work that has put you under stress. Your spouse may have an additional workload which puts more home and family responsibilities on you. Look for other alternatives first, such as additional, temporary household help, more time for yourself (a lunch hour with friends, rather than errand-running), or negotiating time off with your boss after completing a major assignment.

Returning to Work

A number of fears about returning to work after an absence are genuine. Can you survive an interview? How will you manage the home and children? Who would want to hire someone who has so many responsibilities outside the job? Here are two examples of women who are ready to return to work, but are experiencing doubts. Discover how they solved their problems.

Jane's Story

What you reveal at a job interview about your family obligations could jeopardize your chances for the job; but you need to know if your potential employer can be sympathetic to your needs. Read Jane's story. How would you approach the job interview?

Jane has just separated from her husband. She hasn't worked in seven years and she needs a full-time job to support herself and her two children, ages seven and four years old. Until the birth of her older child, Jane worked for five years in the fashion field, continually climbing the career ladder. But tackling job interviews in today's tight market intimidates her, and she is not sure how to approach a job interview. How honest should she be about her children's health? They were sick 25 days last year with the usual childhood illnesses. Would openness about her family obligations jeopardize the possibility of her finding a suitable job?

Rebecca responds:

Jane knows she is a good worker. She knows that despite the demands of her family, she will take her work seriously. She, therefore, should level with the interviewer. She should be forthright in explaining her home responsibilities to the potential employer.

Jane should also question the duties and responsibilities of the position and find out exactly what the day-to-day tasks and activities are. For example, will there be any daily, weekly, or monthly deadlines? Are some seasons busier than others? Are there certain tasks that could be done at home as well as in the office? Will she be expected to put in overtime?

Jane also should try to size up the office situation. Are there other employees likely to have the same concerns that she has? Or is it a competitive atmosphere where there is no concern for the individual or family? Jane must also carefully examine her home situation. While it is necessary that she stay home the initial days of a child's illness, there may be a babysitting agency or woman who could watch the child until he or she is well enough to return to school. If money is a problem, Jane could trade services in kind, e.g., go grocery shopping for the woman (perhaps an older woman) in exchange for babysitting.

Jane needs these answers in order to determine if the position is flexible enough to meet her personal needs. At a particularly painful period in her life, Jane needs an employer who is sympathetic and understanding of her situation. She does not need to feel torn between her job and home responsibilities.

Jane should point out many possible arrangements to the interviewer to demonstrate her thoroughness and seriousness about her responsibilities—both at home and at the office. In spite of some "handicaps" she must be assertive enough to "sell herself" as being the best candidate for the job.

Michele responds:

Rebecca! Isn't that being naive? And you, a woman in the working world! Jane has little pertinent or relevant experience and has not worked for seven years. In a one-hour interview you expect her to digest detailed duties and job responsibilities, make mental gyrations on how to accommodate her home and work schedules, and be assertive enough to sell herself as the best candidate for the job. Talk about superwoman! Then to top it off, you advise her to detail her limitations to the interviewer, and try to work out arrangements that would suit *her!*

As the saying goes, the end must justify the means. Jane must do what she can to get herself a good job. Her personal life should not enter into the interview. After all, she does not know that her children will be sick as often in the coming year as they were last year, or that she will have babysitting problems. Why think up problems for herself? Jane must be realistic—she must do what she can to anticipate possible problems on the home front and plan for them. However, she must concentrate on *positives* in the interview: her past work experience, education, and abilities.

Once she gets the job, the pressure is on. She must work very hard, make herself indispensable, and hope and pray her children do not get sick immediately. She will then be in a better position to negotiate leave and alternative work schedules. If she is as responsible as she seems, she will be able to juggle both—once she gets a job.

Rebecca and Michele

We have shown two approaches to a common problem. One stresses Jane's concern with her home responsibilities. The other advises that Jane emphasize her professional qualifications in an assertive way. As with most human relations, a middle-of-the-road approach might be most practical and productive.

How Jane approaches the interview

"I saw your ad in the weekend paper, and I would like to apply for the position of buyer and fashion coordinator in junior sportwear. I have an AA degree in this field and worked for five years in this capacity. I left work seven years ago to raise a family. Now circumstances have made it necessary for me to return to work. Even though I have been out of the job market, I have kept up with trends through reading in the fields of management and fashion and I have many creative ideas that could be used to benefit this store.

"I am also very concerned about the well-being of my children, and it might become necessary for me to take time for these responsibilities during the day, for unexpected illness or appointments. If the store is moderately flexible about time on the job, I will make up any hours by taking work home or staying later when necessary to meet deadlines. Please understand I want this job, and I feel very confident that I would be very good at it. I offer hard work and experience. In return, I need the assurance that I will be allowed some reasonable flexibility to attend to my children's needs.

Kathy's story

Kathy's children are seven and nine. They are healthy, active children. Their schedules are hectic with each of them involved in several after-school activities. Kathy does part-time volunteer work in the elementary school two mornings a week, is treasurer of the PTA and is moderately involved with a philanthropic organization. She and her husband share in some household work, but she is the home and family manager.

Kathy is relatively satisfied with her life but finds that with the children at school she has more free time. She and her husband have also been concerned about continued rising prices. Her husband suggests that she return to work.

The idea of reentering the work-world is appealing to Kathy. She knows she would enjoy the adult company and financial independence, and she liked her work as an illustrator. But she has several doubts about returning to work. The following discussion ensued between Kathy and her husband, Bob:

Bob

You complain that you are bored with your organization work and with housework. You've also been putting the pressure on me to put money away for college for the kids, and a retirement plan for me. What you could earn would easily allow us to save, and raise our standard of living a little. We could even afford to hire someone to help with the housework. You would be home every night to check on the kids' homework and other needs. You have commented to me numerous times that you don't see the kids from morning till night anyway. I think you're hesitating to return to work because you're afraid to go through the process of job-hunting and interviewing.

Kathy

You're right, I am. But that's only a small part of it. I don't even know what to look for or where to look. I haven't used my skills in 10 years. There are many changes in my field. The demand for an illustrator is negligible, and I have no idea what the pay is these days. Don't forget that we would still have to pay for a sitter in the afternoons from 3:30 to 6 P.M. I don't know how I'd get the kids out in the morning and get myself out, too. And keeping up with the kids' needs is a lot more than checking their homework in the evenings. You forget I have to carpool them several times a week, not to mention doctor's appointments, shopping, and meal preparation. I can't imagine what would happen to the house—even with someone else doing the cleaning. I think it's impossible.

Commentary

Kathy and Bob both make good points. The decision is a tough one. There are several factors and options they need to consider before making a final decision:

- How much training, if any, would Kathy need in order to successfully reenter the market? If the demand for general illustrators is poor, she might consider training in a specialized field, such as a medical illustrator. The time and money invested now might make a large difference in future job possibilities and salary. She could enter a training program on a part-time basis, thus giving her some extra time at home and negating the immediate need for costly sitters and household help.

- What other costs would be involved in Kathy's return to work? In addition to household help, they must compute commuting costs, lunches, and some new clothing. Hidden costs must also be considered, including less time to seek out bargains and grocery specials and to do household repairs and maintenance. And likely, her working will put them in a higher tax bracket.

  A word of caution: the "cost-to-work" argument has frequently been used to keep mother at home. A husband who feels threatened by his wife's work may use this argument to prevent upsetting the family balance. The cost-to-work argument is also a good excuse for a woman who has ambivalent feelings about going to work. This argument, however, does not take into account the promotions and salary increases which will probably ensue. If a woman wants to work, the cost-to-work argument should not weigh heavily in her decision.

- How will family management change? Kathy correctly pointed out that the kids' needs do not fit neatly into the evening. Someone must be available to them all the time, with the crucial period being from 3:30 P.M. on. Kathy can arrange car pools to meet her more limited schedule by finding others to drive one way if she picks up on her way home from work. Neither Kathy nor Bob included Bob in necessary changes. Bob might be able to help prepare breakfast in the mornings while Kathy dresses. Bob might also be able to pick up car pools on his way home. Family management will have to be shared more between Kathy and Bob.

- Who takes care of the house? Children ages seven and nine can take on more responsibility. They can help set and clear the table, make their own lunches, make their beds, and clean up after themselves in the bathroom. Bob can agree to a few more chores. Both can agree to precooked meals to streamline the dinner hour. Home management must also be shared more between spouses.

You might ask, what comes first? Changes in family and home management are never easy. And who and what changes first? Kathy doesn't even have a job yet!

Kathy must concentrate on her job hunt, and her decisions about training possibilities first. She can consider part- and full-time opportunities and determine a "radius" for her job hunt. She can use this transition period to train her family to participate more in family and household management responsibilities and make decisions about hiring sitters and household help.

Returning to Work After a Baby: When Is Best?

The decision about when to return to work after having a baby depends on several variables: your health (both physical and emotional), your office requirements, your financial situation, and the personality of your child. Unfortunately many of us do not have the luxury of making our own decisions. Decisions are usually dictated by the job and the financial situation. However, should you have some options, we recommend a minimum of three months and a maximum of six months. At three months you will most likely have settled into a routine and will have experienced "bonding" with your baby. Beyond six months returning to work becomes more difficult. You begin to feel rusty in your field: you've missed out on events at the office. Most importantly, between eight and 14 months your baby will probably experience separation anxiety. It is therefore best to settle your baby in a child-care situation by six months. If you return to work when your baby is going through separation anxiety, make sure there is plenty of overlap between you and the sitter so the baby has time to get to know her.

Your decision also depends on the personality of your child. You might have a fussy infant demanding your attention and draining your energy with erratic sleeping and eating patterns; you might have a contented infant who almost immediately falls into good patterns. You may feel guilty about wanting to get away from a fussy infant by returning to work as soon as possible—or guilty about leaving that sweet, contented angel. Or you may be just too tired to start coping with both work and home demands.

Below you will find some of the advantages to going back to work when the baby is three to six-months old:

- Baby does not seem so fragile (has gained weight) and has started to respond.
- If you are breast-feeding, the baby will be starting solids at about six months.
- If baby is colicky, it will most likely be over by six months.
- Baby will more likely be sleeping all night—or most of the night.
- There is adequate time for bonding—you and the baby getting to know each other.
- You have had time to regain your own strength.

Saturday Night Out

You are getting ready to go out (with a date or spouse). Your children cling to you begging you not to leave and accusing you of never spending time with them. What do you do? Whether you work or not, children often don't like it when their parents go out for the evening. You have the double guilt in this situation because you are not there during the day. You can't let your children dictate your life, yet you want to make sure that you are spending as much time with them as you can. Examine the situation:

1. Do you feel you have been giving your children enough time? Maybe you just spent a full day at the museum, or took them to a movie yesterday. Or, have you been out of town all week?

2. Let your children know that you are an individual and you have rights too. After all, they go to Johnny's house to play. They have fun at Susie's birthday party. You want to go out also.

3. If your child is old enough, give her a calendar so that she can see some time allocations. Mark down the time you plan to spend with her and the time you plan to go out. For example, "Thursday night I will take you bowling. We will spend all day Saturday during the day together. However, Saturday night I am going out. The day is longer than the night, so we will have more time together."

4. Make sure that your sitter is reliable and trustworthy and the children like him. Make sure that your sitter does not "sit." Discuss activities

to do with the children such as reading stories, playing particular games, and baking cookies.

5. Your children may wonder where you are going. Tell them what you plan to do for the evening. Indicate that it's adults only wherever you are going. Maybe you can bring them back a little something, e.g., candy from the party, or popcorn from the movie.

6. Saturday night television for children is usually not dependable. Having a video recorder so they can see children's films while you are out can be a special treat.

7. Make sure that your sitter has a phone number to contact you. However, don't let him give it to your children unless you are willing to be disturbed. Children will use any pretext to call Mommy and Daddy.

Above all, don't get into a hassle with your children. You have a right to a life beyond them. Be very firm about your going out. Don't feel guilty when you do. But make sure they will have special time also.

Single Parents

The information on child care and home management in this book applies to single parents as well as to dual-career couples. As a single parent, however you do not have the advantage of sharing everyday child-rearing and home management demands. Thus, your time is even more limited and the demands seem greater.

Based on experiences with single parents in our workshops, we strongly suggest that you build a support network for yourself. Find someone who has children close in age to yours, then trade off to give each other relief. In many instances singles hesitate to trade off or make exchanges in kind (you take my clothes to the cleaners, I'll take your book back to the library), because they fear undertaking more than they can handle. They fear they may be taken advantage of, or that the arrangements just may not be worth the hassle.

If you find yourself with these attitudes, examine them carefully. Remember that a support network does more than take your books to the library for you. A support network can share some of your emotional problems, too. Even if you do not feel comfortable sharing your feelings, just the knowledge that others have similar problems—that you are not alone—can be a tremendous boost. We *urge* you to develop a group of friends with whom you can trade off and exchange favors in kind.

Finding the right support network may take some effort. Many communities have organizations especially for single parents, with activities built around parent-child activities. Parents without Partners, a national organization is one. Don't think that everyone attending these activities is looking for a date or that you will be "on display." By attending these activities you will meet people of the same sex and opposite sex who can become your friends. Also try checking the list of parents at the day-care center or your child's school.

Many parents, both married and single, try to be "super parents" to their children to make up for their time away from home. The need to be a super parent is especially strong among singles because of the absence of one parent. If you are attempting to be a super parent, you are heading for disaster. By placing unrealistic demands on yourself—both physically and emotionally—you are bound to be overwhelmed by stress, fatigue, and even anger and resentment toward yourself and your children. Find a relative or friend of the opposite sex who can be a role model for your child.

Travel on the Job

Your job requires travel . . . warm places, night life, scenery, skiing, or none of the above! Travel can be fun or it can be a dud. Before accepting a job, consider the travel issue:

- How much travel is required?
- How often?
- Can trips be made in a day?

You'd be surprised at what you can do. (Rebecca went from Washington, D.C., to Waterville, Maine in one day, efficiently conducted a four-hour meeting and she did not stay overnight. She also made it to Seattle and back within 24-hours—leaving Washington, D.C., at 9 A.M. and returning at 7 A.M. the next day. You need stamina for a schedule like that; you also need to be organized for the business you conduct on travel.)

Most important you should prepare your children for travel. Tell them where you are going, what you will be doing there, and when you will be back. Also:

- Take younger ones to the airport if they have never been before.
- Illustrate a little storybook for them about your trip.
- Discuss what you expect of them when you are gone.
- Call home often—it's worth the expense.
- Bring your children something from your travels.

Home management

- Can your spouse run the car pools? Can you trade days with car pool mates?
- Try a taxi service to pick up your children if no other arrangements can be made.
- Your spouse might need extra help at home. Hire a woman from one of the local babysitting services. She can even spend the night and help during the morning rush and the busy dinner hours. You don't have to worry as much about her relationship with your kids since your spouse is at home.
- Try to make sure the refrigerator is stocked before you leave.
- Be sure that your Home Management Notebook is accessible. If the person in charge is not your spouse, you should have the following information for the caretaker:
  1. Your phone number during travel workday and hotel phone number at night
  2. Phone number of nearest relative
  3. Name and number of pediatrician
  4. Note on medicines or allergies of your child
  5. Medical authorization slip with your signature allowing the physician to treat your child. (Check with your pediatrician or local American Medical Association on what type of authorization is needed in your state to enable your child to receive medical treatment when you are not there.)

For single parents:

- Can your child sleep at a friend's house? If you have several children of different ages, you will have to parcel them out to several friends.
- Perhaps a single friend in your support network can stay at your house.
- Hire a woman to come to your house. Try to have the same person each time you travel.

How much travel is too much?

You must be the judge. It is typical for children to complain when a parent is leaving. Don't feel guilty. But ask yourself:

- Is my traveling upsetting to their routine? What can be done to help them adjust better?
- Are there particular problems at home which need special attention?
- Do I spend a lot of time with them when I am at home?
- Is my spouse overloaded? Maybe I can call in extra help.
- Is the traveling too demanding on my energy?

We feel that day trips, although tiring, are usually manageable. If you find yourself on overnight trips more than half the month, you should reconsider the situation. If you have travel a quarter of the month, be cautious and alert to problems which might crop up at home.

Why Not Fun?

We talk about having fun. How long has it been since you have had fun? How long has it been since you:

- had a candlelight dinner with wine and soft music at *home* with your spouse?
- roasted marshmallows at your fireplace?
- baked cookies?
- went roller skating?
- had a picnic during the winter in your playroom?
- went to a disco?
- went to the theater?

- took a hike in the woods?
- went to the circus?
- rode a roller coaster?
- walked along the beach?
- went to a museum?
- rowed a boat?
- played hide and seek?
- did sommersaults?
- jumped rope?
- went bowling?
- played tennis?
- took a sunbath?
- laughed at something funny?

It's difficult to be spontaneous when you are so busy. Schedule it and do it!!

Postscript

We have tried to be brief, informative, and very practical. In order to offer information, advice, and solutions, we have perhaps concentrated on the negative rather than the positive. But after all, you don't need help when things go right!

We hope that ten years from now there will not be a need for a book like this. We hope there will be changes in the work world such as flexible hours, job sharing, more part-time opportunities, cottage industries, and other accommodations to help support wholesome family life. Also, we hope that there will be equal employment opportunity for men and women and increased options for quality child care. We hope that "balancing" being parents and having a career will no longer be necessary.

Our Parents with Careers Workshops are continuing. If you are interested in participating or being trained to present them, please write to our publisher. Please also write to us with any solutions that have worked for you in balancing parenthood and career. We wish you well!

Index

Related Books from **Acropolis**

PARENTING

The Parents With Careers Workbook: *Everything You Need to Succeed*, Rebecca Sager Ashery and Michele Margolin Basen, $6.95.

Motherhood: *YOUR First 12 Months*, Deborah Insel, $11.95 in hardcover and $6.95 in trade paperback.

The Father Book: *Pregnancy and Beyond*, Rae Grad, et. al, $17.50 in hardcover and $8.95 in trade paperback.

Parent Tricks of the Trade, Kathleen Touw, $9.95 in hardcover and $4.95 in trade paperback.

FASHION

Working Wardrobe, Janet Wallach, $14.95.

The Extra Edge: *Success Strategies for Women*, Charlene Mitchell and Thomas Burdick, $14.95 in hardcover and $8.95 in trade paperback.

Big & Beautiful, Ruthanne Olds, $16.95.

COLOR

Alive With Color: Tap the Power of Color in Your Life, Your Home, Your Wardrobe, Yourself, Leatrice Eiseman, $18.95.

Color Me Beautiful, Carole Jackson, $14.95.

HEALTH

Dr. Neumann's Guide to the New Sexually Transmitted Diseases, Hans H. Neumann, M.D. with Sylvia Simmons, $12.95.

INSURANCE

How to Protect What's Yours, Nancy Golonka, $11.95 in hardcover and $6.95 in trade paperback.

Available at your local bookstore. Or send a check for the list price plus $2.00 shipping and handling for each book to:

Acropolis Books Ltd.
2400 17th Street, N.W.
Washington, DC 20009

About the Authors

...ctorate degree in social work. She has had a ...n research and evaluation, psychotherapy, ...evelopment, community organization, and grant ...ocal, state, and federal levels in health and social ...velfare, genetics, staff development, and drug ...ks full time at the Department of Health and ...Drug Abuse, Mental Health Administration. She ...clinical social work practice. She is co-founder ...arried and has two young children.

...masters degree in Public Administration and ...ve experience in program planning and develop-...rant and contract management, workshop and ...and editing. Her fields of expertise include drug ..., the needs of the elderly, family therapy, child abuse and neglect, and community mental health. Ms. Basen is a former employee of the Department of Health and Human Services in the Alcohol, Drug Abuse, Mental Health Administration. She is currently self-employed as a private consultant. She is co-founder of Parents With Careers. She is married and has three young children.